How To FORGIVE
When You DON'T
Know How

OTHER HEALING COMPANIONS

Good Grief Rituals
How to Break Vicious Circles in Your Relationships
The Secrets of Wholehearted Thinking

A HEALING COMPANION

How To FORGIVE

When You DON'T

Know How

JACQUI BISHOP, M.S. & MARY GRUNTE, R.N.

PHOTOGRAPHS BY RICHARD GUMMERE

Station Hill Press

Published by Station Hill Press, Barrytown, New York, 12507.

Text and cover design by Susan Quasha.
Photographs by Richard Gummere.

Distributed by the Talman Company, 131 Spring Street, Suite 201E-N, New York, New York 10012.

Library of Congress Cataloging-in-Publication Data

Bishop, Jacqui
 How to forgive when you don't know how / Jacqui Bishop & Mary Grunte
  p. cm.
 ISBN 0-88268-142-7: $7.95
 1. Forgiveness. I. Grunte, Mary. II. Title.
 BF637.F67B57 1993
 158'.2–dc20   93-4788
             CIP

Manufactured in the United States of America.

Contents

Acknowledgments

We are grateful to a considerable number of people without whom this book would not be what it is. Our heartfelt thanks go to the following:

- First, as always, our loving, patient, and very forgiving families, who sacrificed time and attention to support this project—and who, of course, have challenged us to learn forgiveness on a daily basis.

  —Leon J. Grunte, who gave above and beyond the call of duty, especially in helping to care for Doris Woods, Mary's mother.

  —Jeanne and Rogers Bishop, for unconditional love and support.

- Our contributing writers and idea people who on very short notice were kind and brave enough to share their own stories and wisdom with us. These contributors include: Jay Albrecht, Barbara Baxter, Diana Calder, Father Denis A. V. Carter S.S.C., Gordon Clark, Joann Deutsch, Jonathan Forester, Rabbi Joseph Gelberman, the Gentle Giant, Leon J. Grunte, Herb Hadad, Jeff Halvorsen, Kate Hammerling, Lyalya Herold, Rosalie Joy, Barbara Hoberman Levine, Alexandria Rane, John and Elizabeth Sherrill, Laurie Stibbards, Corrie Ten Boom, Betty Tihansky, Irene Tomkinson, David Tomkinson, and Helen Zeitlin.

- Landmark Education Corporation, whose flagship course, The Forum, has been healing families for many years, creating forgiveness as both possibility and reality in thousands of lives, our own included.
- Ken Binney for being, as always, an invaluable coach, cheerleader, herald, and promoter of Inner Family Healing.
- Eric Berne, father of Transactional Analysis and Game theory; Stephen Karpman for his brilliant Drama Triangle technique for analyzing Games; as well as Dan Casriel and Frankie Wiggins, whose New Identity process reveals projection so powerfully.
- Joy Davey and Laurie Stibbards, whose loving welcome to their community, Shalom Mountain Retreat Center in Livingston Manor, NY, led to many of the stories contributed.
- The whole gang at Station Hill Press, especially George and Susan Quasha, Cathy Lewis, Julie Parisi, and Anastasia McGhee, whose judicious red penciling, good direction, respect for the creative process, and appreciation of the practical aspect of book writing have been tops.

Foreword

Philip Zimbardo, Ph.D.

Imagine the human mind as a "little shop of horrors," a kind of Smithsonian Institution, where the Main Wing is filled with the relics of all the injustices and harm you've experienced in your life. Each exhibit depicts your memory of what someone did—or failed to do—that hurt you. Brightly illuminated by the glare of your resentment, every exhibit has a sound track echoing with angry, accusing voices. Adorning the walls are horrible instruments of punishment and long lists of penalties to be exacted from your wrong-doers. And coating everything is a thick, clinging residue of self-pity that keeps you from moving forward to the New Futures Wing, where the exhibits are filled with pleasure, joy, and the myriad delights and fascination of the Human Connection.

Can you imagine what it might be like to visit—or worse—be locked permanently inside of such a chamber of ill will? For those of us who have been unable to forgive others for real or imagined wrongs, that chamber exists within us. That chamber of Ill Will is our own mind.

And what a price we pay for maintaining such a museum of resentment! This negative construction of one's past not only sustains anger, bitter rumination, repressed impulses, and seething hostilities, it also turns the mind destructively against itself, thus fracturing the Human Spirit and straining the bonds of all relationships.

The simple, yet profound message contained in this dynamic book by

Jacqui Bishop and Mary Grunte is that the entire edifice described above crumbles in the face of forgiveness. Forgiveness transforms the passion for punishment into passion for life and creates the dignity that comes with pardoning our enemies.

This truth is illustrated in carefully chosen case studies and personal recollections, which recount how people, through forgiving, have cleared away the debris of resentment that cluttered the path to their inner harmony.

Readers are treated to an unusual synthesis of modern therapeutic ideas explaining how and why forgiving works magic on the psyche and the soul. These ideas are centered around the concepts of Inner Family Healing and spiritual healing that comes from recognizing the ultimate forgiveness modeled by Jesus Christ.

But beyond the conceptual orientation, the wisdom the authors offer is *practical*. We learn how to cut through the myths that get in the way of adopting a forgiving attitude. We learn tactics for forgiving that we can master easily. Easily, because the authors so clearly delineate the truth that through forgiving others, we forgive ourselves, we gain in self-esteem, and we free our own spirit to soar to new heights. The key to a *new you* is forged in the crucible of forgiveness.

There's no time to waste: *Now* is the time to prevent the pains of the past from distorting the joys of the present and undermining the promise of the future.

The vehicle for realizing these changes in your attitudes, feelings, and actions is forgiving love—the driving force of this powerful book.

1

*What the reasoning of the heart lacks
in logic, it makes up for in results.*
Merry Browne

Introduction
Forgiveness as an Act of Self-Esteem

Forgiveness is ultimately only common sense. Revenge may be sweet in prospect, but it sours in the stomach. Hatred eats away at body, mind, and spirit. Holding resentment requires energy that would produce more joy if directed elsewhere.

In addition to being sensible, forgiveness is one of the best bargains on the planet. Not only does it affirm, strengthen, and free us; it also opens the heart, instructs the mind, and establishes us as winners in the world of the Spirit. Countless stories testify to the power of forgiveness to diminish or eliminate physical symptoms of prolonged resentment, which can include cancer, chronic patterns of accidents, headaches, arthritis, gallstones, and perhaps even senility.

But forgiving is easier said than done. It's especially difficult to forgive people we think have wronged us when we were too small to defend ourselves. Where deep wounds are concerned, the release of anger and resentment happens in slow stages, on many levels, and sometimes only through a transcendent or peak experience of grace.

And even after we forgive—feel it, act on it, reconcile—we still don't understand it. Forgiveness is, ultimately, a mystery.

Mystery or not, in the struggle to let go of persistent anger, we continue to reach for understanding, and we do find that it helps. Electricity has defied scientists' attempts to define its essential nature; nevertheless, our partial knowledge enables us to turn on lights in the darkness. Similarly, even if we cannot yet divine the essential nature of forgiveness, we can learn enough about how forgiveness works to practice and be illumined by it.

It is our purpose in this book to contribute to such learning and practice as a way to open some doors, perhaps lead you through them, and point the way to further healing. We do this by examining the elements and dynamics of forgiveness—players, pieces, possibilities, and processes by which people have succeeded in forgiving.

To clear the way for this understanding, Chapter 2 challenges over a dozen major beliefs—all distortions or fantasy—that keep people from forgiving. For example, the phrase "forgive and forget" is largely inappropriate where forgiving is concerned, both before and after forgiving has occurred.

In Chapters 3 and 4, we explore what forgiveness is by examining who forgives and who is forgiven. Here is where we introduce the concept of Inner Family Healing, which provides a particularly powerful mechanism for forgiving *ourselves*, perhaps the most problematic component of pardon with which we must deal. Chapter 5 proposes a model of forgiveness, which we call the Forgiveness Pipeline. It consists of three major parts: stages of resentment, the turning point, and stages of pardon. One of the important aspects of this model is that it makes clear the truth that forgiveness can be completed with or without reconciliation, with or without a renewal of love or contact, depending upon the situation and parties involved. Finally, against this background, we also examine the phenomenon of projection, so crucial to the process of sorting through issues of responsibility.

Chapter 6 proposes a way to create a vision to draw one toward forgiveness, even if the means to realize the vision don't yet seem to be available. Chapter 7 explains powerful techniques for releasing the springs of forgiveness and Chapter 8 contains stories from people who have experienced forgiving and being forgiven. These stories testify that forgiveness is a constant; like water, it exists for us whenever we choose to find it, and when we thirst and drink, it is the element that makes us grateful to be alive.

We recommend you read the book more than once, mainly because the part of you that wants to hold onto your resentments will try to block your understanding. Sometimes the prospect of giving up treasured positions that make others wrong feels like dying—even though, as you will see, it is entirely life giving.

Sages through the ages have asserted that the longest journey by far is the one that takes us from the head to the heart. We believe forgiveness is one of the shortcuts and therefore operates to some degree in every successful life. Rage attaches us to the object; it nails our foot to the floor, so to speak, so that at a certain point, we can progress no further in our lives. Forgiveness dissolves such nails, freeing us not only to walk, but to run, dance, and fly.

A final note: A few years ago, we were given the inspiration to establish a College of Forgiveness, an environment where "walking the talk" could become an obtainable reality for all. The idea makes sense to us, although such a college may never include a campus. We have colleges for nursing, engineering, literature, fine arts, mathematics, and making war, but forgiving as a practical skill, one of *the* central, ego-challenging acts of self-esteem required for living a fulfilled life, remains neglected even by our seminaries.

This book is our first step in establishing the curriculum for that College of Forgiveness. We invite anyone interested in shaping and bringing that vision into the present to write or call us. In the meantime, peace, Shalom, and God bless you.

Jacqui Bishop and Mary Grunte
Box 97, Bronxville, NY 10708
914-997-9611

2

What Forgiveness Is NOT
Myths About Forgiveness

Why don't we forgive? Much of what makes it difficult to forgive others is that we haven't forgiven ourselves. But even more important, few of us truly understand the nature and meaning of forgiveness. Rather, we labor under a whole pile of misconceptions or myths about what forgiveness and being forgiven means. Instead of freeing ourselves to forgive, we stand bound and paralyzed because we think forgiving means we have to do, be, suffer, or believe something we couldn't bear. Here is a baker's dozen of the most common misconceptions:

1. I can't forgive because I can't forget.
2. If I forgive someone but don't feel it, then I'm being phony.
3. Some people don't deserve to be forgiven.
4. If I forgive, that means I'll have to trust the person.
5. Asking forgiveness means saying "I'm wrong and you were right."
6. Forgiving someone tells them they can go out and do it again.
7. Forgiving and asking forgiveness are signs of weakness.

8. I need my anger to stay safe; if I give up my anger, I'll be helpless and defenseless.
9. If I give up my anger, then the person will get off scot-free.
10. People who love each other don't have to ask for forgiveness.
11. I can't forgive until the other has confessed, is really sorry, and won't do it again.
12. If I've forgotten it, it means I've forgiven.
13. If I say "I'm sorry," the other person should forgive me.

Do any of these apply to you? If so, you may be in for some relief. Read on.

To forgive and forget means to throw
valuable experiences out the window.
Schopenhauer

MYTH 1

I can't forgive because I can't forget

We've all experienced the nagging—sometimes insane—preoccupation with the pain and rage of an intimate wound. Short of physical pain, nothing else so commandeers our attention. As long as such obsession persists in our consciousness, we have not forgiven. To be free, we need to put that negative focus behind us.

But obsession is not the same as recall of facts about actions and their consequences. We *need* to remember what happened both before and after forgiving is complete. We need to remember the wrong to begin with, because if all we have is free-floating resentment, if we don't even know what we're angry about, it is difficult to focus well enough to forgive. It is extremely difficult to release something when we don't even know we're hanging onto it.

We don't believe most people should forget after they've forgiven either. Almost every wound that requires forgiving also contains important learning—learning that carried a high price tag. Not that we must recall all gruesome details, but it's kind of like turning manure into fertilizer. Memory is what weathers the manure pile of pain into something that provides rich fertilizer for bountiful harvest later on.

What *can* be forgotten is the emotional charge connected with the memories. Like the pangs of childbirth, once the miracle of forgiveness has arrived, the burden of pain can be fully released, completed, and allowed to pass away. The matter is then "off one's mind."

MYTH 2

If I forgive someone but don't feel it, then I'm being phony

It is common to make a decision to forgive intellectually, but be emotionally unable to make it real to ourselves.

One person whose mate ran off with another had previously experienced the release of forgiving and growing. Building on that experience, the person made a deep commitment right then and there to forgive the mate, and it simply wasn't true to say this person felt peaceful and had truly let go—angry and helpless, betrayed and abandoned, suicidal and murderous were more accurate. The commitment to forgive ran well ahead of this person's emotional and thinking processes.

Nevertheless, because the commitment was there, the person was already moving on the forgiveness track, and so in one sense it was as good as done.

In this respect, forgiving isn't a feeling; it's an act of will. That means the decision to forgive can be made based on nothing more than common sense about the cost of hatred, and a willingness to shift as the strength and freedom to do so are given.

MYTH 3

Some people don't deserve to be forgiven

Sometimes a person's crime against another is so incredibly heinous that forgiving seems inconceivable. There are mass murderers by whose command millions were tortured, murdered, orphaned, and widowed. How can a Jew forgive Adolph Hitler? How can a Russian or Ukrainian forgive Lenin or Stalin? How can survivors of severe sexual abuse forgive the Satanic cult members who brutally violated the trust of care to which every child has a right? The abusers have neither suffered nor repented of their abominable actions and, given the chance, would probably continue perpetrating them. They seem less than human.

Whether it's in a hundred lives or one that a person has caused pain, our cry "they don't deserve to be forgiven" rings out in anguish and rage.

The problem is that the very words demand that we *spend energy* holding the other in the wrong.

There's another approach. One proponent and practitioner of that approach is Rabbi Joseph H. Gelberman of the New Seminary in New York City. He lost his entire family—wife, child, and parents—to the Nazi Holocaust, and he has stated to hundreds and hundreds of people that he has *let it go*. He says:

> Most of my colleagues brought Hitler with them when they came here to this country; they were constantly expressing anger and

9

hostility, and it eventually killed them. But I wanted to make sure when I came to this country that he could not kill me, too.

I cannot forgive Hitler in the name of my wife or my child, or my parents, but I can choose to live for them, not for Hitler. Instead of the anger and hostility, I put on the joy that my family was cut off from, that they were entitled to. I resolved to fill my life with the good they should have had.

It wasn't easy, of course. We are trained to be angry when we experience loss or pain, and letting go of the anger took years and years of thinking and praying. But this helped me, and perhaps it will help others: Moses gave his farewell address to the Israelites, saying: "I have spoken to you about curse and blessing, about life and death. I say to you, Choose Life."

So I chose life. The anger didn't help—we have new Nazis right now in Germany today. If we concentrate on ourselves, however, and on joy, peace and harmony, there would not be such things.

Deserving forgiveness isn't the issue. In fact, the Greek word for forgiveness actually means "let go of"—no more, no less. Ideally, someone who has wronged us feels regret and is willing to make restitution. But many offenders don't choose to do so and blithely live their lives as if we didn't even exist. The hard truth is, whether they do penance or not, the one who pays the price for our own unforgiveness is us, not the other person.

MYTH 4

If I forgive, that means I'll have to trust the person

Here's an illustration of how people can get stuck in unforgiveness
when they confuse forgiveness with trust:

> I used to forgive my husband when he did hurtful things, but his
> behavior never changed, and I got angrier and angrier. Whenever I
> forgave him, all he did was go out and do it again. I couldn't trust
> him.
>
> Today I can't forgive my husband for cheating on me. Heaven only
> knows who he picked—I've been scared about getting AIDS or warts.
>
> He says he's sorry for what he did and I believe him, but it doesn't
> stop him from blaming me for everything else he does. The way I see
> it, if he could find what he thinks is a good reason to cheat once, he
> can find a good reason to do it again, and I don't want to get had
> again. It makes me feel like a fool. I'll forgive him when I know he's
> trustworthy.
>
> I don't like the current situation, but I'm committed to my children's
> well-being; I can't carry the financial load myself, and so we need my
> husband's support. I also love him. I don't know how I am going to
> deal with living with someone I can't trust, and I'm angry about that
> too.
>
> Somehow, if I'm going to stay in this marriage, which I intend to
> do, I have to figure out some way to work out an understanding of
> what we're agreeing to so I'm not scared all the time that I'm going
> to get shafted.

You can hear the struggle she's having; it's a power struggle in which a part of her is demanding that he change—become trustworthy—before she will forgive. In effect, she is conditioning her forgiveness on his being trustworthy, and that keeps her trapped.

It will help her to learn that forgiveness and trusting are different from one another, and both are different from reconciling.

- **Forgiving** ultimately means giving up the investment in staying angry and taking vengeance, by returning abuse directly or indirectly, e.g., continually badmouthing the other person.

  Forgiveness is complete when the memory of the incident no longer carries an emotional charge.

- **Trusting** is expecting someone to behave in a certain way because they say they will or they represent themselves as that kind of person. If someone does not keep his word, does not abide by his contract, then trusting him isn't appropriate. *Trust, once lost, must be earned back.*

  Trust is restored when expectations and behavior have matched for a long enough time to create confidence in *both* people that certain expectations will be fulfilled.

- **Reconciling** means recommitting to an agreement that has been broken. Either the agreement gets renewed as originally understood, or it gets rewritten to articulate revised expectations. In either case, it expresses the commitment to an ongoing relationship.

Reconciliation is complete when both parties are in harmony with one another.

Reconciliation is something that depends on both parties being willing to make an emotional investment and take the risk of trusting again. Thus, it goes a step beyond healing the forgiver to healing the relationship.

Most unforgiveness accompanies a power struggle in which the victim demands the other person change while they themselves do not. The rationale used by the victim is that the other person did the wrong thing, and therefore the victim is blameless and shouldn't have to do the changing.

MYTH 5

Asking forgiveness means saying, "I'm wrong and you were right."

This power struggle often centers on differences over what each person considered appropriate in the circumstances—you should have done such-and-such or "any fool would have known better." Here's an example:

> When Hal expressed distress that his withdrawal in pain hadn't been noticed, it sounded to Pat like an angry complaint against her that she and others had failed to intuit what he needed, and she felt manipulated and angry. She said she wouldn't be held responsible for mind-reading and that he should have figured out what he needed and asked someone. Hal said he didn't want anyone to read his mind; he was just expressing some sadness and simply needed to be heard—and by the way, she should have noticed. He acted offended, and he referred to Pat's response as sadistic. He had no awareness of any anger on his part. Who was right? An observer in this story saw merit in both positions, and the debate continued.

In fact, the debate about who was right or wrong wasn't relevant. Forgiveness has nothing to do with right and wrong. The only reason forgiveness is needed is that someone is holding onto anger or hurt. You can forgive or ask forgiveness if the other person was wrong and you were right or vice versa, or if you were both right or both wrong. Asking for forgiveness means asking the person to give up staying angry and give up the "right" to punish or act vengefully. *That's all.*

Forgiveness cleans the slate so that both people can be okay, both people can "win," both people can communicate afresh. That's not possible where vengeance and withholding remain available options.

If this is the myth that hangs you up, notice that being right matters more to you than being truly at peace.

MYTH 6

Forgiving someone tells them they can go out and do it again

This fear of appearing to condone the unpardonable stops many people from forgiving both themselves and others. We know an alcoholic, a young woman from a dysfunctional family. She is now in AA, but there have been moments when, filled with rage at her spouse, she took it out on her kids, screaming at them and hitting them. She's been terrified to forgive herself for fear she will simply go out and do it again. She also believed that even God would not forgive her.

But one cannot use unforgiveness to control behavior—one's own or that of another. In fact, unforgiveness may even evoke the behavior feared. Whatever you resist persists. In any case, even if the person goes out and does it again, that has nothing to do with forgiving. *Forgiveness in and of itself is for the forgiver, not for the forgiven.* It frees the forgiver from replaying the hurtful scene over and over and from the need to take an emotionally costly defensive or offensive stance toward the offender. It stops the power struggle that underlies so much unforgiveness, and it raises the appropriate question: assuming this person won't change, what will *I* do to deal with their behavior?

*Men with clenched fists cannot
shake hands.*

Sufi Teaching

MYTH 7

Forgiving and asking for forgiveness are signs of weakness

"Forgiving is weak is one of the hit tunes of the ego" was the comment made by one young man, whose story follows:

> I was unfaithful to my wife and she knows it. I struggled for a whole year to ask her to forgive me, and every time I went to do that, instead of asking her to forgive me, I kept saying "I'm sorry for what I did, but you drove me to it by accusing me of molesting our children," and that wasn't true. I thought if I really asked her for forgiveness, it would leave me totally impotent. It would put all the power in her hands. It would make me a wimp—and that was one thing I wouldn't risk. So I wouldn't forgive her for being angry at me. And that way I didn't have to ask her forgiveness for what I'd done.
>
> I had a picture of my clenched fists: In one I held my outrage—how dare she accuse me! In the other hand, I clutched my shame—how could anyone forgive me?. When someone said, "Why don't you open your hands and put your outrage and shame down," I made the shift. I was able to look into my wife's eyes and ask her to forgive me, because I truly regretted my actions—and I took responsibility for them. She didn't make me cheat on her; she couldn't have made me do it if I hadn't chosen to do it myself. Now that I have actually stopped lying about who was in charge, I feel honest again—not great, but at least not lying.

Anyone who has walked down the forgiveness trail knows that there is always a point where, if we ask for forgiveness, we could be rejected.

Risking that rejection is only for the brave, for it requires us to lay aside the mask of our pride, our main protection against abandonment. Such an act is a far cry from the apology that comes from fear or weakness and is designed to mollify the other. Both true forgiveness and true repentance arise from and produce self-esteem, a desire to affirm and strengthen the truth in oneself. They are actually a manifestation of creative power.

> *Only heaven means crowned, not*
> *conquered, when it says "Forgiven."*
> **Adelaide Ann Procter**

MYTH 8

I need my anger to stay safe -
if I forgive, I'll be helpless and defenseless

We knew a man many years ago who ran a half-way house for ex-convicts in a ghetto in a large metropolitan area. When confronting the question of whether or not to forgive a person who had threatened his wife and children and done extensive damage to the residence, he could not bring himself to forgive because, he said, "I can muster the strength to deal with this person only if I have enough rage. Without my rage, I am not strong enough, and I won't take that risk." Given the very real dangers of the situation in which he worked, he had to maintain his rage pretty constantly, and it was not surprising to learn a few years later that he was prostrate with a stroke.

Understand that there's nothing wrong with anger. When we recommend giving up anger toward someone, we're not saying anger is bad. On the contrary, anger, like all the emotions, serves a positive purpose. For example, it gives us physical energy to fight when we're threatened, and staying power when we need to remain determined. It signals our intellect when something's wrong that needs to be fixed. The issue is not whether anger is good or bad—it's whether we use it to empower ourselves or to keep ourselves from moving on.

There are three things to understand about anger, safety, and forgiveness.

- *A person can forgive someone without forfeiting the right to use anger in self-defense.* Forgiving means letting go of anger and angry thinking about specific things in the past, not relinquishing the power derived from using anger appropriately.

- *It is true that the adrenaline from intense anger helps a person to fight, but it is not true that one has to have that kind of anger to be strong enough to win.* In fact, anger can contribute to losing, because some people have trouble thinking clearly and creatively about alternatives when they're angry.

  The person who says, "I need to stay angry at this person to stay safe," has assigned magical powers to anger, the power to keep harm at a distance either by frightening people away, or by keeping herself alert to the possibility of betrayal or attack, or by simply presenting a wall of resistance to whatever comes her way.

- *When anger is driven by intense fear and is seen as the key to survival, it must be fed increasing quantities of stimulation in order to persist.* This amounts to having a monster for a watch dog. It demands more and more food and gets bigger and bigger until everyone in the house it was designed to protect is also subjugated to it and may even be used as fodder to keep it alive.

  To put it another way, such anger takes on a life of its own, and it and the adrenaline it produces drive our lives, much the way alcohol and drugs do. Rage-aholics and other people addicted to control are generally victims of this kind of imbalance. People who won't give up this kind of anger frequently die of its effects. Heart attacks, strokes, cancer, and a host of other fatal diseases have all been attributed to the tension it creates.

*If I owe Smith ten dollars, and God
forgives me, that doesn't pay Smith.*
Anonymous

MYTH 9

If I give up my anger, then the person will get off scot-free

When we are young, we lack the psychological defenses that later shield us from adverse emotional energy. We are very vulnerable to emotional negativity. Someone who is chronically angry, silently or otherwise, can create such emotional tension in a house that we can hardly bear it.

It's only natural for children to conclude anger is a form of punishment. Accordingly, when we feel wounded and want to even up the score—create a more equitable balance of pain—it's not surprising that we use anger, rage, and hatred as weapons. It was painful to us as children, and we assume it can create pain for others when we're adults.

While it can and does create pain for our children, just as it did for us, our adult anger has no such power over adults who don't live with us. We cannot do other adults any harm with anger alone unless they specifically allow it. The only adult we can truly harm is ourselves—the offender skates off into the sunset, unscathed, and perhaps even gloating, knowing that we are so thoroughly, helplessly, caught in our own helpless rage against them.

> I was so angry at myself. I was angry that I hadn't seen how out of whack the relationship was. I was almost as angry at myself for not having stood up for my values. I had sold out.
>
> It took me forever to get angry at Andy, but then when I finally did, I was furious. Not a single commitment remained unbroken, and I was determined Andy would pay for it.

The worst part of it was that Andy was rich, happy, remarried—and totally out of reach. I was absolutely helpless to inflict harm in any way whatsoever, much as I thirsted to do so. All I had was my rage, and I was absolutely determined to send as much of it Andy's way as I could. And so I did.

I oozed hostility and cynicism. I fairly crackled with indignation. I was in a constant stew. My arthritis flared, and I had constant headaches. I couldn't sleep for hating. It wasn't until someone who had been a friend to us both remarked that I looked terrible that I suddenly snapped to attention. I'd always been conscious of my good looks, and that person couldn't have gotten my attention any faster any other way if he'd yelled, "Fire!" I looked in the mirror, and I looked 20 years older than I am. I was actually allowing Andy to rob me of 20 more years. Need I say more?

It is easier to forgive an enemy
than to forgive a friend.
William Blake

MYTH 10

People who love each other don't have to ask for forgiveness

When people first fall in love, any small transgressions seem to get swallowed up, not only in passion and the excitement of discovering and being discovered, but also in a reservoir of trust in each other's good intentions—in the assumption of good will. We are temporarily swept away by the child's dream of loving and being loved unconditionally.

People cherish the illusion that such idyllic romantic love can persist indefinitely, but life makes it painfully evident that it cannot. First there's the problem of trivia. When two people live independently without having to deal with the practical questions of who does the cleaning, laundry, or bills, the picture can be romantically idyllic. But let them move in together, and they find even sharing one bathroom can be hell. A thousand small items can act on the psyche like the drip, drip, drip of Chinese water torture.

In addition to the power of the trivial to dement us, there is the vulnerability of being close to another person. Whoever wrote "Love is never having to say you're sorry" was either naive or lived life alone. Who is in a better position to wound—knowingly or unknowingly—than the person to whom we have opened our heart most deeply? How could we possibly live and work together without letting one another know that we regret insensitivities and petty self-indulgences, not to mention major betrayals?

Romantic love and forgiveness, rather than being redundant or mutually exclusive, are absolutely essential to one another, for we all betray both ourselves and others daily, and the resulting pain and guilt must be healed if we are to keep it from destroying that which we hold most dear.

Myth 11

I can't forgive until I know the other person is really sorry and won't do it again.

It feels awful to be on the rough end of the stick and know the other person doesn't even care—or takes satisfaction in our pain. How can we forgive someone who feels no remorse, no pity, no love, no pain? It isn't fair. Why should we have all the pain and the other person have none? I thought that person cared for me.

If I've wronged you, you want to know in some way that I feel bad that you feel bad, that I am willing to feel the pain of having let you down, of having been less than I could be. If I have betrayed a vow or solemn understanding, I can't toss off an "I'm sorry" and expect you to find forgiving me a simple thing if there's no evidence that I have repented or paid any kind of price.

The problem is that staying angry until I repent is a no-win situation for you, because it puts you at the mercy of my behavior. You are inextricably tied; what has already been painful once continues to be painful again and again. The power struggle to make me love and care for you the way you want can never be fully won except from your own inside.

MYTH 12

If I've forgotten, it means I've forgiven

"It's OK. Just forget it. I don't want to be angry, and I don't want you to get into your guilt. I'm really just tired of the whole thing. Let's just *forget* it." And the person really does let it disappear from conscious awareness. A few weeks later, it has sunk out of sight and out of reach.

Or has it?

There are two kinds of forgetting around forgiveness. One of them arises from love and understanding, and from knowing one is safe from significant harm. It carries no emotional charge, no weariness or irritation. On the contrary, it is accompanied by pleasantly warm feelings of compassion and/or good humor regarding the offender's obvious regret and eagerness to make restitution. The good feelings can also have something to do with having seen the problem coming, adroitly sidestepping the damaging salvo, and moving back in to care for the person.

In the other kind of forgetting, the offense remains available whenever needed to justify revenge. A man named John Berry said "Pardon your neighbor before you forget the offense," knowing we are sure that what disappears from conscious awareness without being forgiven is sure to sink into the swamp of stored grudges, there to ferment until payback time.

MYTH 13

If I say I'm sorry, the other person should forgive me

"I *said* I was sorry, what more do you want?" Some people believe that acknowledging they have transgressed in some way fulfills the offender's obligation in a matter and should finish it. "Why beat a dead horse? What's done is done. I know it's not fair, but neither is life."

But saying, "I'm sorry" is often like throwing sugar on top of cow manure—the cow pie still isn't palatable for the person who's had to eat it.

People who feel wronged want some kind of justice—the blindfolded lady with the scales evened up. That's the virtue of an eye for an eye—at a minimum, the initial victim isn't alone in being a loser. Better still, the victim wants to be able to move out of the position of loser into the position of winner; in human terms not being the loser usually means making the other person the loser. Even win-win thinking, which represents a step beyond the win-lose axis, usually looks like compromise.

What we are proposing represents a step beyond win-win, beyond any sense of winning or losing at all. What forgiveness is really about is wholeness—a distinction in which winning and losing are largely irrelevant concepts.

3

Forgiveness is a funny thing.
It warms the heart and cools the sting.
McKenzie

What Forgiveness Is

We actually cannot articulate the exact nature of forgiveness, because the more deeply we delve into it, the more levels, subtleties, and possibilities we find it contains. It is an energy of some kind. It is a decision. It is a feeling. It is a mystery far exceeding the ability of mere words to describe. However, many of us can relate to the *experiences* associated with forgiveness:

1. *Connectedness,* openness with oneself and the other
2. *Acceptance* that someone close who hurts us can also love us
3. *Clear individuation,* knowing viscerally that another person's action defines who *they* are, not who *we* are
4. *Peace,* thoughts of goodwill
5. *Freedom* to choose to be close or distant with that person
6. *Ability to serve* the person without resentment
7. *Pleasure* in their good fortune
8. *Equality,* a sense of being physically the same size as the person who hurt us, also equal in other ways
9. *Release* from self-pity; wisdom from the experience; in some cases, the ability to feel light or even laugh at what happened and what we made of it
10. *Self-acceptance,* affection for ourselves, compassion for our pain.

These do not define forgiveness *per se*, only the results of forgiveness. What they do establish is that forgiving is powerful, desirable, and worth pursuing.

Webster's Dictionary defines the verb *forgive* as follows:

i. **To give up resentment against or the desire to punish; to stop being angry with; to pardon.**

ii. To give up all claim to punish or exact penalty for (an offense); to overlook.

iii. To cancel or remit, as a debt, fine, or penalty.

Despite the apparent clarity of this definition, this describes what people *do* when they forgive; it doesn't describe the power that dissolves the hatred.

Here are a few other things we can say about the nature of forgiveness:

- The decision arises out of a commitment to be at peace with oneself and others.
- The action involves letting go of a fixed negative attitude toward someone.
- The results benefit the person who does the forgiving more than the person being forgiven.
- The process occurs on a number of levels in a sequence that appears to be unique for each person and sometimes for each occurrence.
- The accomplishment appears to be an expression of self-worth.

While none of these definitions nails down the nature of forgiveness, each certainly establishes forgiveness as something desirable. To give you a better chance of releasing forgiveness into your own life, we now turn to questions of who does the forgiving and who actually gets forgiven.

4

Who Forgives? Who's Forgiven?

This section examines the question, "Who forgives?" from four perspectives. First, we explore the dynamics of the Inner Family, because it offers some possibilities for those of us who feel so stuck in our fears, anger, or pride that we don't believe we could ever truly forgive a person. Second, we explain Game theory, which is appropriate to consider for those situations in which we unknowingly carry responsibility for the problem. Third, we look at the dynamics of grudge collecting, which signals Games and so often accompanies unforgiveness. Finally, we examine the phenomenon of the offender who cannot forgive.

The Inner Family and Forgiveness—
The Grownup as Forgiver

You, like everyone else, have an Inner Family, comprised of a Grownup and a variety of Inner Children. What do we mean by the Inner Family? "Inner" refers to what exists in a person's internal awareness, as opposed to what exists outside the body and can be seen by others. "Family" refers to patterns of thoughts, feelings, and behaviors that resemble a family structure of personalities and interactions.

You may not have thought of having an Inner Family in just those terms, but we can all identify words and phrases that run through our brains to

> *Forgiveness is the answer to the*
> *child's dream of a miracle by which*
> *what is broken is made whole again,*
> *what is soiled is again made clean.*
> **Dag Hammarskjold**

tell us how we are or should be thinking, feeling, and acting in response to what's going on in our lives. When we listen carefully to these words and phrases, they begin to sound as if they are coming from particular personalities with distinctive characters. As we continue to observe, it becomes clear that some of these characters sound adult while others sound childlike. Moreover, their patterns of internal communication— both negative and positive—recall our own upbringing.

Let's take a closer look at the Inner Children and the Inner Grownup that comprise this Inner Family.

The Inner Children

These Inner Children have different ages, characters, ideas, tastes, and even genders. It is these Inner Children who carry the pain and make the decisions connected with early trauma. The Inner Children never get any older than they are, but if your Inner Grownup learns to take care of them, they can be healed of the wounds sustained when you were small. Until that happens, they often insist on occupying the driver's seat of your life, especially when they feel threatened. As most of us can attest, having a 3- or 6-year-old in charge is a tough way to make a living, raise a family, or handle a crisis. These little ones do their best, but there's no way they can adequately substitute for an experienced, mature Grownup. The Inner Children are trapped in the past. In effect, each lives—for good or ill—in a time capsule encased by your history.

34

The Inner Grownup

The Grownup is the part of us that is legally responsible for taking care of business, taxes, family, and self in the outside world, and emotionally responsible for taking care of the Inner Children in our inside worlds. Unlike the Inner Children, the Grownup continues to age chronologically, and to benefit from experience in the here and now. The Grownup is also the only one with the capability of entering into the Inner Children's time capsules to help clear away the painful elements there and to refashion the environment into a joyful and healing one.

In a properly balanced adult personality, the Grownup functions as "Captain of the Will"; that is, master of the power to select, commit to, and pursue a particular direction for our lives, in concert with or in contradiction to our emotions or preferences. In other words, the Grownup is the part of us that is ultimately responsible for exercising the power to choose at each decision point.

In this capacity, it is the Grownup who sets the goal of inner peace and freedom, and who moves resolutely toward forgiving, no matter what feelings, emotions, and thoughts may seem to impede that progress. And feelings, thoughts, and emotions do impede that progress, at least temporarily. The reason is that Inner Children, just like normal, healthy biological children, compete with the Grownup for control. Their tastes and desires often differ from one another and from those of the mature adult body in which they reside, and, like normal "outer" kids, they want what they want when they want it.

More important than mere taste is the Inner Children's attachment to survival decisions. They have tried to preserve their mental, emotional, or physical existence by thinking or feeling a certain way, and they believe if the Grownup violates those decisions, they'll die. Here are just two examples of those kinds of decisions:

- **Feelings**. Some of us grow up in households where all the adults think if they feel scared, they'll be helpless. What they are most scared of is being scared. So instead of feeling fear, they decide to feel angry—at least that feels powerful instead of helpless.

  The child watching the adults knows about their fear intuitively, so he takes it as a lesson: "It must be dangerous to show or even feel fear , so I'll never be scared; I'll get angry instead and stay that way until things change."

- **Thoughts**. In other households, what seems to count is being right—or at least, not being wrong. If a person can prove he is right, he doesn't have to eat crow—be rejected, ridiculed, or abandoned. Only those who are right seem to have any power, be winners, be respected, be worthy, be loved, be free, be SAFE. Therefore, the child decides being right is a survival factor and learns to defend his position whether that position was right, wrong, or even irrelevant.

> *A wise man will make haste to forgive,*
> *because he knows the true value of*
> *time, and will not suffer it to pass*
> *away in unnecessary pain.*
>
> **Samuel Johnson**

Such survival decisions powerfully alter a person's life generally and interfere with forgiving specifically. It is for this reason that we often want to forgive yet feel completely incapable of doing so.

The Grownup has the power to forgive nonetheless, and we're not speaking of false or empty pardon. We're speaking of an act of authority.

Here's a metaphor to illustrate how it works. The Grownup is not only a part of the personality, it is also a role, a function—we might even say, an office. In the same sense as a person assumes the office of the president, the Grownup assumes the Office of the Grownup. Now, when the new president of the United States assumes office, he is not a big enough person for the job. In fact no one has sufficient stature when first taking office. For the presidency, the candidate is, at best, a senator or governor who also has campaign experience and a few popular ideas. But a statesman? A world-class decision-maker? Not by a long shot, and every thinking person knows it. Nevertheless, he moves into the office and exercises all the authority associated with being president of the United States. And as he does so, he learns, he makes mistakes, he learns, and he grows.

In the same way that the new incumbent of the Oval Office makes decisions and grows into them, our Grownup can exercise the authority to forgive as an act of will even if it hasn't yet appropriated full personal power, even if the Inner Children have no interest in any kind of forgiveness, simply because the Grownup occupies our Oval Office. That act will then set in motion a train of thinking and feeling events that culminate in complete forgiveness on all levels.

Such acts of will aren't easy to live with in the interim, however, if the Inner Children are still invested in rage and vengeance. To deal with such discomfort, the Grownup can exercise another right associated with our Grownup's Oval Office—the authority to call for assistance from outside forces. So not only can the Grownup forgive, it can also call on a Power beyond itself to assist in the process. It is often only in the shower of grace that we are able to let go of the struggle to be right, only grace that relieves the fear and heals the pain and anger, and grace that creates a new and intimate relationship, if that is appropriate.

Sometimes a problem in forgiving someone else is actually a problem of forgiving oneself. In some cases, both victim and victimizer share responsibility for whatever mess has been created and sorting it all out can get very complicated. To help navigate through the tangle, it's invaluable to know about the theory of Games.

Who's Guilty? Some Games Are No Fun

Forgiving is so much simpler when we can see the "good guy" as all good and the "bad guy" as all bad; alas, life is seldom so simple. Between adults, most commonly both the abused and the abuser bear some responsibility for the mess. Have you ever said fervently to yourself, "This is the *last* time!" and then "How did I get myself in this pickle *again!*" This kind of conversation signals the operation of a *Game*. It is to Games that we now turn our attention.

A technical term coined by Eric Berne, father of Transactional Analysis, a Game is an unconscious and unconsciously driven series of exchanges that end in a Payoff of bad feelings and judgments against self, other, and the world.

Because many resentments between adults relate to the consequences of Games, it makes sense to understand how they work so we can learn to take responsibility where appropriate. This is not a book on Games, however, so we are confining our explanation to this brief section.[1]

Games are played from three main positions—Persecutor, Victim, and Rescuer—which we depict in the Drama Triangle as follows:[2]

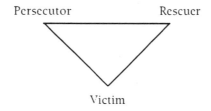

Those who prefer the *Victim* position almost always feel frightened, powerless, and in pain. They continually get themselves into one kind of pickle or another. *Persecutors* tend to feel angry or indifferent. They dish out the pain, continually blemishing situations or people and punishing them for it. *Rescuers* tend to feel superior, right, and unappreciated for all they do. They are typically rushing in on white chargers to save people from their own helplessness or from Persecutors—whether they need to be saved or not.

A Game appears on the surface to be nothing but a power struggle, but it is in fact a carefully orchestrated *collaboration between two or more people for the purpose of exchanging vitally needed strokes without risking intimacy.* The strokes usually begin as positive and always end up as negative. That makes them powerful. It also makes them safe—we needn't get too close, for who would expect us to stay near someone who causes us pain?

A common example is the person who helps (rescues) someone in distress (a Victim) only to discover that person turns around, gets into trouble again and expects the Rescuer to rescue again. The Rescuer then switches to Persecutor—"Shape up, get your act together, stupid!" and the Victim then switches to Persecutor also—"What do you know about it, you arrogant, self-righteous jerk!" This knocks the original Rescuer out of the Persecutor box and down to Victim. They part, each feeling angry and judgmental.

While everybody plays Games sometimes, and everybody hits every position eventually, most of us favor one position over the others, at least behaviorally. Other people can tell us which position it is, even if we don't see it that way.

Three main things to remember about Games in regard to forgiveness are:

1. *It takes two people to open a Game*—one to play Victim and one to play Persecutor or Rescuer, and no one can force either one to play.

2. *By definition, Game players know not what they do.* Games are played from the unconscious.

3. *Only Inner Children play Games,* but the Grownup is responsible for allowing it.

Games Are Played Unconsciously

If the people involved are aware of what they're doing, it's not a Game—it's a conscious manipulation. When the players of a Game begin to comprehend what they've been participating in, they are typically horrified.

If Games are played unconsciously, how can we know we're even playing, much less stop? To become conscious about it, we can ask our friends; they've watched us play time and time again. When we've suffered enough, we'll hear their wisdom. We can also ask ourselves the question, "What keeps happening over and over?" The answer describes the Game sequence.

It Takes Two To Play Games

No matter how hard one player tries to draw another person into a Game, there's no Game if the other refuses to play. This is because opening any Game requires two people, one to play Victim and one to play Persecutor or Rescuer, and no one can be forced to play a Game. So if a Game is played at all, even if the Victim has been deeply wounded, he/she must share responsibility for causing that pain.

Having said that in a Game the Victim shares responsibility with the Persecutor, let us make two crucial points:

1. **There are true victims in this world who are not responsible for their distress** and mustn't be confused with the Victim in a Game. All it takes to make a true victim is an

imbalance of power, especially physical power, and no escape for the weak. Children, especially, are dependent and therefore lack power to defend themselves from predators.

A true victim's Grownup can be in the driver's seat from start to finish and it will not alter the victim's fate. Tragedies such as war, rape, crime, disease, and so on all create victims, and we mustn't compound their agony by insisting they be accountable not only for surviving their pain but for causing it. People tend to blame themselves anyway, and that's never appropriate for true victims.

2. **Neither true victims nor Game Victims are responsible for the behavior of whoever inflicts damage.**
No one has the power to control the behavior of another adult. No one can force anyone else to hit, kick, rape, shout, lie, or drink or take drugs. Without the threat of violence, "You made me do it" is almost always a lie.

This brings us to the third thing to remember about Games.

Only Inner Children Play Games

Remember, Games are played to obtain vitally needed strokes. When an educated, healthy Grownup is in the driver's seat and is meeting the Inner Children's needs, there is no need for Games because there is no need for negative stroking to compensate for any lack of positive stroking. But if the Grownup is off duty, the Inner Kids fend for themselves in the only way they know how.

Faults are like car headlights. Those of others seem more glaring than our own.

Anonymous

It's not surprising, then, that people will seek out someone to take care of them whose character matches that of their original caretakers. The Inner Children, remember, are caught in a time capsule, a theater, where the only film shown reruns scenes from long ago; there's little or nothing in their awareness to let them know reality has changed. They assume things are the way they were when their family was in charge.

When they find such a person, the past and present become hopelessly tangled. Then they get married. No wonder that so many divorcing couples behave toward one another in such bizarre and inconsistent ways. Each one has married the caretaker who failed. If you doubt this, ask each spouse in a marital war to describe their own primary caretakers—mother and father (or, in some cases, a much older sibling or grandparent)—and then ask them to describe how their embattled spouse resembles one or more of their original caretakers.

Often, though one or both people deeply desire to be in a holy and forgiving relationship with one another, they feel a wall of unforgiveness blocking the way. The utmost they can do is tell the truth about being unwilling to forgive. Why? Because the person they need to forgive is not the spouse but the original caretaker. It is the painful bond with that caretaker that needs to be released. Until it is, the spouse can't even be seen, much less forgiven.

Games also become easier to understand when you realize that internally at least two Inner Children are involved in any persistent Game pattern:

1. **The longing, hopeful Inner Child** who persists in the struggle to win love at last from those who should have given it so

long ago. The problem is that this Child keeps picking the same kind of person to get it from and consequently experiences the same kind of lack and rejection. This child was, back then, a victim in the true sense of the word, and continues to be a victim in the Inner Family.

2. **The angry, despairing Inner Child** who gave up on being loved the way it wanted and decided to stay angry instead to avoid the pain. For this Inner Child, the payoff of a Game lies in the opportunity to struggle, rage, and condemn the chosen caretaker and—no less important—avoid the terror of true closeness, which would expose its *imagined* unlovability. As a rule, the way in which this Inner Child punishes both the longing, hopeful Inner Child and other adults is the same way in which this Child was treated by its own early caretaker. This Inner Child perpetuates what was learned from the abuser.

   Even more tragic, this Inner Child is often the one in charge when we are raising our own biological children. Finally on top, we pass on what we hated to those whom we most love.

Unforgiveness can be seen as a power struggle in which both these Inner Children are pitted against "what ought not to be that way." They hold a negative attitude, indictment, or complaint against that original someone and struggle to change the past. We might as well struggle to change a movie on a screen down at the local cinema. The past is what it is.

What we can do is change the present. The Inner Grownup has the capability to enter into the Inner Children's time capsule to satisfy the original unmet need for unconditional love and thus relieve the underlying despair. Once the Inner Children have what they need, the drive for negative strokes stops.

Explained in terms of the Inner Family, forgiveness is complete when our Inner Children:

1. Stop using anger against self or other as a magical way of controlling the past, present, and future.
2. Accept that what happened back then did happen and that they can't change it.
3. Let go of judging it (or themselves) as good or bad—saying that it wasn't fair and shouldn't have happened to them, or that it *was* fair and they deserved it.
4. Look to their own Grownup to supply what that person did not.
5. Surrender authority regarding what happened or didn't happen to the Grownup.
6. Know they can safely have all their feelings and thoughts about that person, knowing that their Grownup will limit their actions to what conforms with their long-term well-being.

But how does one get one's Inner Children to reach this point? If we don't even know what forgiveness is, how do we get our stubborn, proud, wounded selves to make it happen?

Part of the process of healing is learning new behaviors that release grudges instead of storing them.

The High Cost of Grudge Collecting

One of the important signals of a Game, and one of the most persistent patterns of unforgiveness, is saving grudges. A grudge is defined in Webster's as follows:

> i. Sullen malice or malevolence; spite; ill will; **a cherished dislike**; as, an old grudge.
>
> ii. **A reason, cause, or pretext for ill will.**

People collect grudges over a period of time until they have enough of them to trade them in on delivering a whammy to the other person without feeling guilty. We've adopted some terms to express the elements in this process more vividly.

Grudge rhymes with sludge, which aptly describes the atmospheric quality around people who collect grudges. The atmosphere doesn't change until the collector has enough grudges to form into a *sludgehammer*, with which he or she delivers the ultimate whammy *without feeling any guilt*. Sludgehammers can be large or small.

Some people horde grudges the way Scrooge hordes his gold, polishing and counting them consciously or unconsciously, keeping meticulous track of their weight to see if they're ready to form into the sludgehammer. Sometimes this goes on for years until the day they're ready to trade them in on doing something vengeful to the other person.

In the next vignette, we've taken a humorous look at the dynamics of sludging. We all do some of this. To make this truth a little more palatable, we've couched it in the following expert sludger's letter to a young sludger:

Dear Prospective Sludger,

This is my humble offering to all those who would take justice into their own hands.

1. Get the people closest to you—they're the easiest to spot, you can collect grudges faster, and you know exactly how to get 'em.

2. Collect all you can early in the week before they suspect anything. For example:

   —Whenever they leave a mess in the kitchen (that was Grudge #1).

   —When you're watching TV and they bring their noisy friends through the living room, making you miss what must surely have been the most important part of your program (that was Grudge #2. I now had two).

   —They come home at 11:45, slam the front door, and wake you out of a sound sleep (that was Grudge #3). Things are starting to get tricky at this point. The sludge is building, and they're beginning to sense that you're setting them up. You can't be careless at this point.

3. Pick a time when the other person is *fully* occupied with doing something else and ask them to do something for you. Naturally it doesn't get done (I was now up to four grudges).

4. Some grudges are just gifts—careless neglect, such as forgetting to rewind the video (Grudge #5, the sludge was almost slopping over).

No one is ever old enough to know better.
Holbrook Jackson

5. Once you have enough grudges saved up, it's time
   to sludge. You can do a whammy or my favorite,
   which is Slow Sludging.

To maximize the effect of both kinds of sludging, wait for the
weekend, preferably when they're laughing and joking in the kitchen.
Don't take on more than one person if you're just starting out; you can
handle up to four if you've become a pro.

Enter the kitchen, and begin to direct the sludge into the atmosphere generally. It will suppress the energy, and pretty soon, the
secondary targets will become depressed and leave, which breaks up
the chirping. Then begin leveling complaints at the primary target
person, using a voice that combines whine with moan. Keep it up until
they begin to simmer. Then leave them with it, so that when the other
person takes out their sludgehammer, you are safely out of reach (I
personally favor the basement as a place to retire).

Do not under any circumstances allow the target person to reach a
rolling boil, or else it will be there waiting for you when, hours later,
you rise up from the basement. At that point, because they will be at
a higher elevation, you are at a severe disadvantage. Your only recourse then is to puff yourself up like the proverbial monster arising
from the deep. If you're lucky, you may scare the target person away
from the cellar door long enough to make your escape.

Sincerely,
Someone who knows

If you thought this was funny, as most people do, the likelihood is that
you too have sludged on one side or another. It is important to learn about
how you do it.

In addition to Slow Sludging, there are other forms of sludging. One illustrated here is Silent Sludging. We're all surrounded by an electromagnetic envelope that carries an emotional atmosphere, and we can use that for good or ill. Simply directing malice toward another can create discomfort. In Slippery Sludging, the sludger drops bits of sludge to wait, like a banana peel, for the unsuspecting target to misstep. One client as a child actually left her roller skate under some leaves at the bottom of a flight of stone steps. Her father's foot found the skate, flew out from under him, and deposited him on his behind. He didn't know what hit him until long afterward. By the time he accused the culprit, she was long gone and successfully played the "Who me?" innocent.

In sharpest contrast to slow sludging, take the not uncommon case exemplified by Lyalya's spouse who, after years of giving no indication of discontent, says out of the blue one day, "I'm leaving you. My lawyer will call you tomorrow to initiate divorce proceedings." This is an example of someone who's been saving up grudges for years so that when he finally wields the sludgehammer, it is devastating. Here's the story of how she forgave him:

The Monkey and the Banana[3]

The Forum:

At The Forum, as we explored the ways in which we human beings behave, we came to a term called "a racket." A racket was defined as a way of doing or being in which there was a complaint. Then the question was, "What do you get out of a racket?" Well, you get to be right, you get to be superior, you get to be better than someone else, you get to be virtuous, etc. So, what does this racket cost you? Well, it costs you your energy, your health, your vitality, your joy, your freedom, and—in some cases—your life. In order to illustrate this point, the Forum leader told the following story:

How do they catch monkeys in the jungle in this day and age? The hunter brings in a Plexiglas box, which has a small, round hole on one side. Into it he slips a banana. He places the box underneath a tree in which there are some monkeys, then retreats into the distance. Inevitably, one of the monkeys gets curious and comes down out of the tree to explore the situation. He finally puts his hand through the hole and picks up the banana. But when he tries to withdraw his hand, the banana, which is being held horizontally, is blocking the way. The monkey jumps up and down, squeaking and squealing, trying to get free. In the meantime, the hunter appears out of the jungle and captures the monkey. So, the question is, "What did the monkey need to do in order to get free?" DROP THE BANANA.

In an instant, I saw its application to my life. At the break in the morning session, I called my husband. I told him I forgave him. For the first time, I could hear that he was on the brink of tears. He said that he never meant to hurt me or cause me pain, that he was willing to meet with me any time I wanted to talk. We agreed that I would call him and arrange a time.

There was not to be that resolution that I so devoutly hoped for. Forty minutes into a very, very tense and strained meeting, I saw him looking restlessly at his watch. At that moment, I was filled with such total despair that I simply closed my eyes and prayed to God to help me. The answer came clearly. I suddenly felt a bubble of joy rising from the pit of my belly. *"You don't have to change him, Lyalya, all you have to do is forgive him."*

I stood up, kissed him on the cheek, told him I wanted him to know that I wished him well in his life and that I forgave him. Just as I got to the door, he said, "The question is, can I ever forgive myself?" Then he started to say something. I was not sure whether he was unable to forgive himself for remaining in the marriage or for having behaved as he did! I told him that issue had nothing to do with me. It was something he needed to resolve with himself. As I walked out of the door into an icy cold winter evening, I felt absolutely free and happy.

Every time you experience irritation at someone and fail to communicate on the grounds that "It's too much trouble" or "I'm sick of talking about it" or "It won't do any good" or "I don't feel good, but it's not that important," chances are you are minimizing either yourself, the other, or the slight, and storing up a resentment.

Anyone who harbors small resentments against someone else is building a sludgehammer. If you would be truly free and capable of acting in a way that you can be proud of, then trade in your grudges before you have so many that vengeance or divorce seems your only recourse.

The best way to deal with grudges is not to collect them, and the way not to collect them is to communicate about them as close to the time they occur as you possibly can.

If you've already accumulated a horde of grudges, there are a number of positive ways to trade them in. In most cases, the simplest route is simply to call up the person, tell them what you want to do, make an appointment to see them, tell them what you've been feeling and thinking, what you want, and what you intend to do about it. Tell them you forgive them for what they did. Ask for any forgiveness you may want for holding

The noblest vengeance is to forgive.
H.G. Born

anger toward them, for example. Keep going through the process until all emotional charge is dissipated. Other options are contained in the section, *Some Processes for Forgiving.*

When the Offender Can't Forgive—A Look at Projection

One of the oddest things about forgiveness concerns the offender who doesn't forgive. In exploring this vital subject, we focus on divorce, not because it's the only place offenders don't forgive, but because the determination to annihilate the other is so bizarre, so close to love, and so easy to see.

- Take the husband who in his mid-50s takes up with a younger woman and then leaves his wife, whom he then proceeds to destroy financially during the divorce process, systematically and coldly.

- Consider the wife who leaves her husband to be with another man, but even after the divorce is final, continues to abuse and harass her ex with lawsuits, midnight calls, custody battles—even a suit for the custody of the dog, just because her ex loves it.

The pattern has been well known for a long time. For too many ex-spouses, the damage is never enough. It seems as if they cannot rest until their victim is annihilated. Unfortunately, our legal system supports such goings on, making legal between spouses what would be jailable offenses

> *Forgiveness to the injured does belong;*
> *For they ne'er pardon who have done the wrong.*
>
> **John Dryden**

between strangers. The movie, *War of the Roses* depicted it in graphic and hilarious detail. But it's hilarious only when it's happening to someone we don't know. When it's happening to us or someone we love, it's strange and hateful.

What drives such unreasoning hatred? Why does the divorcing spouse— even when happily married to a new love, perhaps raising a new family, affluent, and successful—demand such a price of the person who's already paid so dearly? Only when we see beneath the offender's surface rage to the underlying self-hatred, fear, and guilt does it begin to make sense.

To understand where these factors originate, how they work on the psyche, and what is needed to be free, we need to step back and see what happens as our Inner Family is formed.

When we experience abuse as children, we tend to conclude that it happens because of something shameful about ourselves. It's too dangerous to assign responsibility for the pain to the appropriate parties (our caretakers)—abandonment might follow and then, surely, death. Instead, we assign what we believe causes the abuse to one part of ourselves and reject that part as shameful or even dangerous to be or to express. In other words, we divide internally, magnifying some parts of ourselves as OK and burying others. The more difficult or abusive our childhood was, the more intensely we reject or disown the aspect of ourselves we think is causing the problem, and the more violently—and unconsciously—we struggle against it as adults.

We would "get rid of" the rejected parts of ourselves if we could, but we can't—a good thing, because our original decision to reject ourselves is based on a misunderstanding that we may correct later. In the meantime, however, the parts of us that do the rejecting lie about it; they do everything they humanly can to divorce themselves from any identification with the victimized parts—*Not me, I'm not like that, only other people are like that. In fact, I hate people like that—watch me, I'll prove it to you.*

Not only do we reject these Inner Children internally, we see and reject them everywhere—because everywhere we look, we find people like that. We have a projector inside us that plays the image of the Rejected Child onto those outside ourselves. The fantasy is that if we can shine it "out there," we no longer have to deal with it "in here." *Don't we wish!*

This process of rejecting a part of oneself is referred to in many different schools of thought. Jung referred to the rejected part of ourselves as "the shadow," because it is considered the darker part of a person and for that reason is denied substance. Ronald Laing referred to it as the disowned self.

In Inner Family Healing, we call it The Myth of the "Bad" Child. [4]

Unfortunately, getting away from our own Rejected Inner Children is impossible for three main reasons:

1. We are unconsciously but irresistibly drawn toward what we've disowned.

2. We struggle against being those parts and it is well known that whatever we resist persists.

3. The projector is in our own forehead, so the images we are trying to flee confront us everywhere.

Paradoxically, when we enter into a love relationship, the person we choose to love usually expresses some of the parts of ourselves we rejected. Why do we choose such a person? *Because we need that other part to be whole.* The phrase "my other half" often expresses the truth more precisely than we know.

Once the romantic glow has faded, however, we object to the other person's being the way they are. It seems perverse, but only on the surface; why, having rejected those parts in ourselves, would we accept those parts in another?

We all know couples who exemplify this pattern. Take the Arthur Miller/Marilyn Monroe combination—a very academic, mental person marries a volatile, nonintellectual personality. He is initially fascinated, amused, and enlivened by this person, and then, as the romantic excitement wears off, irritated, and ends up spending a good deal of time making that person wrong for being "too emotional." Or The Odd Couple, like Oscar and Felix—the messy person who marries a neatnik is initially delighted by a new sense of order in the home; six months later the neatnik has been labeled a "domineering, anal-retentive nit picker" and the disorganized free spirit now carries the moniker "Pigpen."

The intensity with which we reject this projected Inner Child depends on how severe our childhood traumas were. The more difficult our childhood, the more likely we are to want to annihilate the part of us we think got us into trouble, and the more likely we are to operate as offender.

This explains the intensity and apparent insanity of unforgiving offender behavior. The offender is desperately, savagely attempting to an-

> *The highest and most difficult of all moral*
> *lessons— to forgive those we've injured.*
> **Jewish Ideals**

nihilate . . . oneself, a part that is feared. In this effort, one can do truly terrible things, with or without provocation. Spouses find themselves totally shut out, the targets of financial holocaust and relentless and brutal hounding, and they don't understand why they are being singled out for such treatment.

Because the projector is in the offender's own forehead, the abuse is never enough. No matter how long one hammers and batters at the spouse, the same picture hangs before one, and the freedom so desperately desired remains out of reach.

Paradoxically, the more the offender is conscious of common decency, the more difficult and savage the behavior may become. On top of the terror of becoming what one fears oneself to be, the offender lays the shame of behaving in a despicable way. There's no way that a woman can look at the father of her children or a man can look at the mother of his children and not know at some level that inflicting unnecessary pain is madness. The spouse's very existence is a reminder, a reproach to the current reality of the offender's offenses. Now the person is caught between a rock and hard place.

The offender who acknowledges his or her behavior as shameful becomes, in a way, as rejectable as the victim. The toughest forgiveness challenge may not be to forgive those who've wronged us, but ourselves for wronging them.

Because the Inner Child in the driver's seat wants to avoid that confrontation at all costs, the offender takes refuge in further denial and punishment in an attempt to drive the other to behave in a way that justifies one's abuse. Only if the offender can make the spouse an object of contempt can he or she feel exonerated.

What can the offender do? In some ways the most miserable of creatures, the offender hosts a war in soul, mind, and body in which terror, rage, guilt, fear, and pride all battle against the truth.

Normally, it is said, the offender never forgives. This is because one has no power to heal as long as one's only experience of the Rejected Child lies outside oneself, in the image projected onto the spouse.

Nevertheless, those projections can be reclaimed, and peace attained. There is inherently nothing wrong with Rejected Inner Children, and if a person is willing to face the risk that the same unlovely characteristics projected onto the other may also lie within oneself, one can discover the true beauty of these Inner Children. The Grownup can then ask the Inner Children's forgiveness for allowing the persecuting behavior to go on. This clears the way for one to forgive oneself.

Let us say this again: Offenders who choose to seek the truth can find it, and the truth does heal. Slowly, painfully, one can break through the granite of denial, until the dawn when one realizes that the stone has been rolled away from the tomb and one has finally awakened to a new life of freedom and, finally, peace.

Although we can guarantee that this healing can happen for those who desire it, the process by which it happens is unique for each seeker of truth. In the next section, we look at the anatomy of forgiveness, and especially at the points at which a person turns from anger toward pardon.

5

The Anatomy of Forgiveness
The Forgiveness Pipeline

Forgiveness runs through phases that are useful to look at when we are considering how to arrive at a peaceful place in ourselves. These phases are as follows:

1. Resentment
2. The Turning Point
3. Pardon.

Each phase is composed of its own parts or stages through which we pass on the way to completion.

Stages of Resentment

The resentment phase includes the original injury and initial response to it, as well as the longer term settling into attitudes toward the offender. These occurrences fall into three main stages—the acute, the nursing, and the chronic:

- **Acute stage.** The acute stage comprises: (1) the original experience of injury in the here and now; (2) fear, pain, and anger heightened by earlier events; and (3) the initial refusal to accept what has happened and to struggle against the other person or the situation.

The person experiences feelings initially as numb or chaotic, then confused and fearful, then angry—or all of the above all at once. The acute discomfort demands an evening of the scales.

- **Nursing stage.** In the nursing stage, the person goes into a process of intensifying the feelings of anger and eliminating the confusion of other feelings and thoughts. Basically, the victim defines the persecutor as wrong, gathers evidence as to why that's so, and proceeds to cement that thinking into place by rehearsing it with anyone who will listen. There is no attempt in this stage to distinguish actual accountability; rather, the focus is on making oneself *right* and the other *wrong* and on elaborating vengeful scenarios.

- **Chronic stage.** The chronic stage involves: (1) hardening attitudes developed in the nursing stage, and (2) reshuffling belief systems and identity to conform to the energy of resentment. People in the chronic stage:

  a. Define themselves in terms of the power struggle, e.g., I am a victim, I am unlucky, I am unlovable;

b. Generalize the offense, that is, blame and distrust all similar people as being perpetrators, e.g., if my mother hurt me, then all women are sadistic. If my father left me, then all men leave. If a white person cheated me, all white people are dishonest—or all black people or all Arabs or Jews or French or Italians and on and on...

c. Reorganize their life processes to reflect distrust of such people. In such reorganizing, withdrawal is common, not so much to express fear but to reject "those people."

It's important to note that this hardening is often unconscious. It's as if once the initial computer program has been written in stage 1 and debugged in stage 2, it simply operates, the original injury often forgotten. The anger ferments underground; only the resentful behavior remains evident, sometimes only to others.

The time to intervene for healing is obviously before this chronic stage is reached, for when the resentment drops down into the unconscious, it is far more difficult to unearth and heal. However, it remains active over the years, later yielding the bitter fruit of illness and depression, and appearing on our faces for all to see.

The Turning Point

What turns a person from resentment toward pardon? What moves a person to forgive when forgiving doesn't come easily?

> *Know all and you will pardon all.*
> **Thomas A. Kempis**

Here are some of the crucial thoughts that people say helped move them toward forgiveness:

1. **My resentment is costing me too much.** Holding resentment costs us dearly in terms of health, energy, love, peace, and future possibilities.

   Health: Arthritis, high blood pressure, cancer, strokes, and migraines are some of the most common conditions that can have roots in unforgiveness.

   Energy: Attention takes energy, and it costs us energy to pay attention to another person's behavior so we can continue maintaining an attitude toward them.

   Love and peace: Being at peace with all persons doesn't mean trusting all persons. It means being at peace and trusting *ourselves* with all persons so that we don't have to divide ourselves to be with them. When we hold anger toward someone, especially someone we love, we close off a part of ourselves not only from the other, but from ourselves as well.

   Future possibilities: What we refuse to forgive, we tend to perpetuate in our lives. The spouse who won't forgive the ex-partner will tend in the next relationship either to marry or to recreate the same problems, or to create other problems through trying to dominate the other person so he or she doesn't think, feel, or behave like the last one.

2. **I can't control the other person no matter how long or how much anger I hold.** The perpetrator has moved on and will live well regardless of whether we forgive them or not. The only person impacted by our resentment is ourselves.

3. **There's gold in this incident for me and I intend to get it.** Extracting the gold involves committing to learning from the pain by analyzing how we could have avoided what happened and changing our behavior and thinking where called for.

   For adults, this includes analyzing to see if a Game was going on and identifying any ways in which we ourselves might have participated in inviting or encouraging the painful behavior (as in the Games described above).

4. **My hatred is turning my own future dark.** When a person hangs onto anger, negativity eventually colors all feelings and begins to force a downward turn of our whole history.

5. **I'd rather spend time on what gives me joy in my life.** When we file the experience away as learning, refuse to plug into its old emotional charge, and turn our attention to what creates joy and satisfaction in our lives, the wrong we've suffered begins to shrink, the investment we have in staying angry no longer seems worth it, and we can move toward resolution.

6. **God allowed this to happen for my spiritual good, and I choose to claim that good.** In many scriptures, the Almighty is quoted as promising good out of evil. "All things work together for good to those who love and serve the Lord" is only one of those.

This is a spiritual perception. Not everyone can identify with this turning point of view, but it may prove important to know that many people, even people who have suffered enormously, have concluded that all experience can provide soil for producing good fruit. Here's one example:[5]

A man stole money from my husband's business, and largely as a result, the business failed and bankruptcy ensued.

My husband took a good new job, but it allowed us to see one another only on weekends. I hated the separation. I felt angry at being forced into these unwanted changes and I blamed the man.

As was my habit, I buried my anger. While researching and writing my book *Your Body Believes Every Word You Say*, I discovered that burying emotion is a prescription for disease and could lead to a major unwanted illness. Having learned from a 15-year encounter with a brain tumor, I also knew that what I think and say influences how I feel physically and emotionally. I knew that underneath the hate and the anger was the most basic emotion of all—my sadness. And I felt my sadness. I cried a lot!

One day, however, I began to see that the situation was actually producing some gains in my life—for example, I no longer feared living alone. In fact, I was enjoying the freedom to do what I wanted, when I wanted. I could say I hated my new life or I could be really grateful for the lessons I learned and for the release from my former fear. I could Choose To Be Happy—no matter what!.

Recognizing what I gained made it easier to forgive the man who stole from my husband.

I am grateful to have found the key to turning life's lemon experience into sweet, thirst-quenching lemonade. I believe I've learned the lesson now, since by the time you read this, my husband and I will be together full time again. This whole experience confirmed my belief that LIFE IS FOR-GIVING!

7. **The log in my own eye outweighs the splinter in theirs.** Where projection is concerned, there's always a denial of our own shortcomings. A softening of attitude comes from realizing that we too have a killer within, a person who if pushed far enough could give the person a run for their money on any scorecard at all.

I was one of those children that other kids picked on. Where I grew up in the islands, if you get hurt, it was your own fault, and that's what my mother believed. So on top of being beaten by my schoolmates, I got punished at home for crying about it. My grandmother used to tell me to forgive them, and I did my best, but it was very hard. The worst time was when they dragged me into a hole and left me there to die. I really thought I would die there. Hours later, someone came and saved me, but that was the end of forgiving for me. For many years after that I lived with pain and anger in me because I hated what they did to me, and I felt the rage was my only protection. I lived with that resentment for a long time.

Only when I made a terrible mistake myself could I begin to let go. At 18, I had a miscarriage. It was my fault because I didn't fully understand how an expectant mother needed to take care of herself. My husband blamed me, and he was partially right. I begged him to forgive me, but he refused. I had a lot of time to think about what it was to have done something so bad that it took someone's life.

Mutual forgiveness of each vice
Such are the gates of Paradise
William Blake

When my husband finally forgave me, I felt as if a huge weight had been lifted from me. That's what enabled me to forgive my schoolmates. I never thought I had anything in common with them, but this and other experiences showed me how difficult it is to really know right from wrong when one is young, small, and relatively powerless.

As bad as any of my problems have been, I feel the worst thing we can experience is failing to forgive. I also learned what an amazing gift forgiveness can be. Forgiving and being forgiven not only felt good. It allowed me to create a whole new chapter in my life.

Stages of Pardon

There are three main stages of pardon:

a. **Letting go.** To let go means: (1) to relinquish the power struggle against what happened; and (2) to accept that what happened *did* happen, and there is nothing we can do to change its happening; (3) to divert our concern with what happened into other channels that advance the rest of our lives.

b. **Healing the wound** means grieving—releasing the pain and allowing the grief to flow. It also means taking remedial measures to reduce the pain of whatever situation remains. Such remedial actions include looking for new things to take the place of what was lost.

Healing the wound is partly a function of time, so it can take a while. It is also a function of the perception that who we are and what we have gained far outweigh the cost of the experience.

Healing the wound is complete when we can remember the incident without contracting mentally, emotionally, or physically.

c. **Reconciling** means recreating the relationship, renegotiating its terms, making new commitments to it, and eventually celebrating the learning and growth that came out of the forgiveness crisis.

It's very important to note that *reconciliation takes two.* Both parties must acknowledge the wrong, the consequences, and the pain; the wrongdoer must feel and communicate remorse and then move to make restitution, no matter what it costs in the way of pride. The victimized must choose to risk trusting again.

Reconciliation is complete when trust has been restored.

Remorse and restitution, important gateways to reconciliation, often open only if the wounded person is willing to communicate. Sometimes the offender doesn't even realize the offense has been committed; other times an old resentment has blinded the offender to the importance of the victim to him or her. Even in such cases, however, when the wounded person communicates to the offender that the offender broke a trust and that it caused deep pain, it can evoke profound remorse.

For this reason, it's important that victims not suffer in silence. Hearing the wounded person's agony can be excruciating for the offender, but if that pain leads to remorse, it's worth it. Paul speaks of this in his second letter to the Corinthians, written after hearing about the changes they made as a result of the confrontive first letter he had written:

> Even if I did wound you by the letter I sent, I do not now regret it. I may have been sorry for it when I saw that the letter had caused you pain, even if only for a time; but now I am happy, not that your feelings were wounded but that the wound led to a change of heart. You bore the smart as God would have you bear it, and so you are no losers by what we did. For the wound which is borne in God's way brings a change of heart too salutary to regret . . . . It made you take the matter seriously . . . How your longing for me awoke, yes, and your devotion and eagerness to see justice done . . . although I did send you that letter, it was not the offender [offense] or his victim [the hurt] that most concerned me. My aim in writing was to help make plain to you in the sight of God how truly you are devoted to us.[6]

For situations in which people love one another, this excerpt exemplifies the proper intent of confrontation between victim and offender—it's to put the relationship right. Exactly how that happens in the hearts of those involved is not entirely clear.

Fortunately, we don't have to know precisely *how* to forgive, or even *what* forgiveness is, in order to take the first step toward doing so, which is to develop a vision.

6

*And throughout all Eternity
I forgive you, you forgive me.*
William Blake

Visioning Forgiveness

Like electricity and forgiveness, the power of vision is a mystery that serves us whether we understand it or not. It's simply a matter of understanding how to turn the switch, so to speak. Here is the switch for activating the power of vision:

1. Tell the truth about all aspects of your current state.
2. At the same time hold a clear, detailed, multi-sensory, and emotionally rich picture of what you desire.
3. Continue keeping both these realities in your mind and you will be drawn inexorably toward your desired state.

When we feel angry toward a person we've been close to, what our vision is usually filled with are the experiences of unforgiveness. For some of us, the best vision we can come up with is relief from one or more of the following:

1. *All-or-nothing thinking:* If anything's wrong, everything's wrong. We can't remember or feel good about the worthy things the person is or has done; all we remember is how they don't measure up.
2. *Cutting off:* We feel numb or indifferent towards the person.
3. *Overattachment:* We can't remain calm about any action the person takes; we interpret their every move personally.

4. *Rage, and wanting to hurt:* We want to kick the person in the teeth; we think of physical revenge or even murder.

5. *Repulsion:* The fact they're alive troubles us. We want them to disappear completely from the earth.

6. *Resistance to continued obligation:* We can't care for the person's needs without seething, blemishing, and criticizing them.

7. *Envy:* We resent any good fortune that befalls the person.

8. *Powerlessness:* We feel mentally, physically, and emotionally smaller or weaker.

9. *Self-pity:* We can't see past our own pain to appreciate theirs. We see nothing funny about the situation.

10. *Guilt and shame:* We hate ourselves for feeling so negative and feel ashamed that someone chose to hurt us.

Beyond visioning relief from this list of miseries, there are a number of other ways to create a vision of forgiveness for yourself. The easiest way is to imagine what you would do, feel, and think if you had already forgiven. If, for example, you want to forgive an ex-spouse, you might imagine you and your ex both attending a graduation of one of your children. In this vision, your ex may or may not have changed, but you feel fine—attractive, strong, free, and detached from your ex. Whether your ex is alone or not, friendly or not, remorseful or not, clingy or not, makes no difference to you. You know you were instruments for one another's growth, and that you made the most of the opportunity, whether your ex did or not. You salute that person and move on.

Sometimes a vision of forgiveness is simple freedom. A friend, Barry, said to us triumphantly one day, "Well, I did it, I finally forgave my friend!" "How does it feel?" we asked him. "Great! Like I felt when I quit drinking a year ago. I just let go of something that was gettin' ahold of me." That freedom has become precious to Barry, and today his tilt toward forgiving, and especially praying for people with whom he's angry, has become strong.

When such pictures don't come easily, a deeper but less well-defined track must be followed that has to do, again, with the will. Access to their own willpower can be obstructed by severe early trauma or substance abuse. For some of us, deep and long-standing resentments, especially toward someone with whom we've been close, have formed such a large part of the very fiber of our lives that we can't begin to imagine what it would be like to have forgiven the person.

In such cases it takes more heat than we can muster to melt the ice around our hearts. What it takes is company, comrades, a community of committed companions to align with and encourage us on our journey to freedom.

It may also take an appeal to something beyond ourselves, a Higher Power. The nature of that appeal varies enormously from person to person, but when we are attracted strongly enough by the promise of forgiveness to ask for help, even the faintest hint of turning can open the door for us. Take, for example, the following story:

> Starr Daily was a brutal and dangerous criminal who was thrown into solitary confinement. While there, suffering with cold, fever,

thirst, and hunger, he reflected that his life had been entirely governed by rage and hatred.

As he lay on the floor of this dungeon, he thought about how his whole life had been governed by hatred. Then the question occurred to him, "What if I had loved instead of hated?" Immediately, there came flooding into him the most amazing and ecstatic peace and joy; he experienced for the first time being loved and welcomed unconditionally.

From that moment on, his relationships with every person in prison changed, and he went on to a ministry of extraordinary power and healing.[7]

When we experience Divine forgiveness, we are immersed in a healing balm so nourishing and satisfying to us that nothing else can make us feel poor or demeaned. This power attentively waits for the least indication that we are truly willing to surrender to Love.

So when you are truly up against it, incapable of advancing through the forgiveness pipeline on your own, you can call on the power of Love to make up the gap between what you desire to accomplish and what you can do. You can ask the Holy Spirit to give you the necessary vision of forgiveness, to take your resentments, and to replace them with forgiveness. What have you got to lose?

For every one who keeps on asking receives, and the one who keeps on seeking finds, and to the one who keeps on knocking it will be opened to you. . . .

Matthew 7: 8

7

Minds are like parachutes — they only function when open.

Thomas Dewar

Some Processes For Forgiving

Forgiveness is very personal. There doesn't seem to be any set or right way to do it or experience it. For one of us, forgiving may be simply a matter of declaring, "I forgive you," and it's done. For another, it's a matter of time healing the wound, and one day we wake up and find we'd like to see the person again. For still another, it's a constant sore that doesn't go away, no matter how much therapy, how much crying, how much raging we do, and then suddenly we realize that what's in the way is our own guilt, which we've been projecting onto the other person; that guilt once admitted to, we're free.

More often than not, unforgiveness has something to do with our Family Spell, an old memory picture laid over the present scene, that renders us temporarily incapable of being in the here-and-now. To forgive, we actually need to work with the early memory rather than the person of today.

In this chapter, we suggest ways to go about forgiving that have been helpful to us and others. The basic strategies involve one or more of the following: expressing feelings that have been denied or suppressed, identifying and relieving any fears the Inner Children may have, revealing the Family Spell images that may be in the way, and, finally, surrendering pride. As preparation for any of the following exercises, imagine yourself facing the person you have committed to forgiving.

75

Take a Leap Forward in Time

The following exercise invites you to create a vision of forgiveness for yourself. It is only one of many ways to go about this, but it is a start, and it has proven powerful where reconciliation is possible. First, choose someone who you are committed to forgiving. Then follow this meditation:

Imagine that you are very old. Many of your friends have already passed on.

You are walking through a park in the springtime. The breeze is gentle and the birds are singing their hearts out. Daffodils are at their peak and, with the warming sun, the flowering trees are suddenly blooming, and you are reminded of your youth.

Looking back over your long life, you are aware of having lived fully and well. The pains and the joys have woven a rich tapestry for you, and you have gained wisdom, humor, and a measure of peacefulness. Life seems long and short at the same time, long because so much has happened, and short because you know there's not much time remaining. So you savor this spring day, feeling grateful for every detail of beauty you see as you walk along.

You notice, to the side, sunlight falling on a little curved bench, inviting you to come and sit a while to enjoy the view. You gaze through trees dappled by sunlight, over a flowered meadow, and finally down to a large lake which you know to be deep and clear.

As you approach the bench, you see someone coming down the path from the other direction. This is the person you chose at the beginning of this journey.

You haven't seen one another for years and years. And then the memory comes back, of what happened long ago, and how it was allowed to stand between you for such a long time. You both stop, remembering, looking backward in time.

Returning to the present, you see one another now, at the end of your lives, as you are this spring day. Around you both is a beautiful light, like a mist of gentle affection in which you stand, looking at yourself and this person.

You know you're being given a choice, probably for the last time in this life, to heal the old wounds. The other person knows also. What will you do?

You both move to the bench, sit down, and look out over the lake to the meadow. After some moments of silence, the words come to your mind, "Will you love this person as you have been loved?"

You turn to one another and, speaking from your heart, tell that person, "I want to hear everything that is in your heart regarding us and any unfinished business between us. It's been much too long for us to remain estranged because of things unsaid. We're too old now to play a waiting game."

You listen as the person expresses all that remains to be expressed. When he or she has finished, you say thank you. You then say whatever you need to say to complete this long-standing affair between you.

Write a Letter

One of the simplest forgiveness processes, if not the shortest, is to write the person a letter (which you do not plan to send). The letter should be written for the purpose of helping you establish a new, clear basis for continued relationship with that person. It doesn't matter if the person is living or not.

The letter should express how you feel and why, say what you want, and declare that you now forgive the person.

You have completed the exercise only when you can say the letter is authentic, and you would welcome receiving such a letter yourself. Don't be surprised if getting to that point takes several drafts. Decide whether or not to send the letter only after you're sure the emotional charge is off the matter, that you've said what you mean, that you mean what you say, and you haven't said it in a mean way. Wait three days to confirm that.

If I Could Get My Hands On . . . !

This exercise provides a way to express and let go of all the murderous fantasies you might consciously or unconsciously be nursing. Here's how it goes:

> Picture, about four to six feet in front of you, a miniature version of yourself about a foot high. Get clear that this tiny version of you is absolutely safe from any harm and so are you.
>
> Now, let that image of yourself express all your feelings *fully*. If you want to blow the person up, dismember the other person, melt the person down, picture this image going through those motions.
>
> The actions can be as awful as you want because absolutely no one is going to be hurt. The purpose of doing the exercise is to release feelings, just as one releases pus out of a boil and thus relieves pain.
>
> Direct any anger *outward*. Under no circumstances should you allow this image to turn on itself, you, or any of your Inner Children. That's merely a way to avoid expressing anger at a person when it feels dangerous to do so. If that's what this image wants to do, say no, and keep inviting it to express the real resentment outwardly.
>
> Whenever the image stops being angry, ask, "How do you feel? Do you want to do more? Keep going until you're finished." When the image has finished, ask what it wants now—a hug, a rest, a puppy.
>
> Check out all the Inner Children to see if they also want to express anger or other feelings toward this person.

I Could Just Scream

Taught for years by many therapeutic notables,[8] screaming is excellent for those of us who are angry at someone but not entirely sure why. The purpose of the exercise is to discharge excess emotional energy so thinking and perception can clear up. The drawbacks are that you may get a sore throat and it's very noisy. You'll need a place where you can make a huge racket without being disturbed. If all else fails, go out in a car and, making sure *all* the windows are rolled up, park somewhere along a parkway, hang onto the steering wheel and scream your head off. You can do it alone, or, better still, have a friend come along.

At full volume, scream the first thought that comes to mind about the person. Then the next thought and the next. Better still, think the thought and scream the feeling. But don't get lost in thinking. If you only have one thought, just keep screaming that over and over. Eventually, once you have the predominant thought, you don't even need to think the words. Let the words go and just make sounds, letting the feelings roll through your body.

Don't be concerned about what the specific feelings are as they come up, or why you feel them. Long-standing resentments almost always include pain and fear, broken dreams, and often humiliation. Your purpose is not to sort through the "garbage," but to flush it out of your system.

Express the feelings (rage, sadness, fear) until finished. Then hold your Inner Children and allow the love to flow toward them.

The Inner Children may resist expressing their rage, for example, because "it won't do any good." It's true that it won't change the past, and it's important to know that expressing feelings, especially rage, does not change anything outside ourselves. But that's not the purpose of expressing feelings.

The purpose of expressing feelings authentically is to enable us to discharge them, integrate the stuck energy, and make way for feeling good in the present. And that, of course, is what we're after. Who cares about past injury to us if we feel good and valuable in the present?

If we express feelings and we don't feel any relief, then one of two things is likely: (1) the feelings being expressed are substitutes for the real feelings (e.g., we may be expressing anger but really feeling sadness underneath), and we need to get to the real feelings before we can discharge; or (2) we're using the feelings as a way to make another person change ("If I stay sad (or angry or scared) for long enough, you'll have to do what I want (take care of me, stop hurting me, come back, feel guilty).

If neither of these two exercises does the trick, then we help people examine more deeply the origins of their resistance to forgiving.

When Was the First Time You Felt This Way?

When the Family Spell[9] has been activated, we need to forgive what happened in that original scene before the present-day impasse will start to ease.

So have your Grownup ask the Children when was the last time they felt this way about someone. An Inner Child will remind you by bringing the scene or memory to mind. Don't worry if the response doesn't seem strictly logical at this point. The first memory that comes up may be just a bridge to the one you're looking for. You may cycle back through several such scenes before you get to the original one.

When the memory comes up, have the Grownup tell the Inner Children that they are perfectly safe, that the Grownup is in charge and will allow no harm whatsoever to come to them. Say that you love them and you're not leaving them under any circumstances whatsoever. If you're aware of a lot of anxiety, you might want to call or ask someone to come over and simply be present with you while you explore the memories. Once the Children are reassured, then proceed by asking them these questions:

1. "What do you remember happening?"
2. "How did you feel?"
3. "What did you decide?"
4. "What do you think that did for you then?"
5. "What do you think that decision is doing for you now?" For the other Inner Children? For people you love?
6. "What are you willing to change?"

If I Forgive, Then . . .

Another way to get at what the Inner Children fear will happen if they forgive someone is to complete, in writing, a series of statements, as in the following:

> "If I forgive, then . . . *I'll have to . . .*"
> "If I forgive, then . . . *I won't be able to . . .*"
> "If I forgive, then . . . *the person will . . .*"
> "If I forgive, then . . . *you'll . . .*"
> "If I forgive, then . . . *people will . . .*"
> "If I forgive, then . . . *life will never. . .*"
> "If I forgive, then . . . *no one will ever . . .* "
> "If I forgive, then . . . *God will (or won't) . . .*"
> "If I forgive, then . . . *I'll never . . .* "
> "If I forgive, then . . . *Mom or Dad will (or won't) . . .*"
> "If I forgive, then . . . ."

Keep going until you have several phrases that evoke some emotional response. Then go back to the list and read each one aloud, asking, "and then? and then?" to see what the chain of reasoning is.

Here's an example:

> If I forgive my mother, then she won't feel guilty anymore.
>
> And then? *she'll go away.*
> And then? *I'll be alone.*
> And then? *I'll die.*

So one of this person's Inner Children has it wired up that if he forgives his mother, he'll die. That's the thinking of a very young child and has no relevance in the here-and-now. The Grownup can speak with this Inner Child, reassure the Child that he or she will not die in the here-and-now because the biological mother's job is over—for better or for worse—and that the person has survived. Now the Grownup is both mother and father. When his Inner Child has taken in that information, even partially, the person then moves on to any other statements that carried an emotional charge.

Here's another example that shows sometimes people hold resentment against one person so they won't have to confront another:

If I forgive my father, then I'll have to deal with my mother.

And then?	*I'll be very scared.*
And then?	*I'll have to tell the truth.*
And then?	*She'll be too angry.*
And then?	*She'll give me away and I'll die.*
Is that true?	*No. I, the Grownup, will never give this Inner Child away. This Child is mine.*

How Do I Do to Myself What This Person Did to Me?

Often we are angry at someone else less for what *they* have done to us more than for what we have done to ourselves. In some way or another, the other person has simply echoed or replicated our own self-abuse, and we have blamed them for all of it. This pattern, discussed earlier in this book, is called projection—we *project* onto someone else the responsibility for what we ourselves are doing or have done.

We have one Inner Child who is abusing another, and our Grownup doesn't know it until we see the behavior in someone else and intensify it by projecting our inner war onto them. Then we fight that person, with the combined energy of the enraged Inner Victim striking back *and* the Inner Abuser who is happy to have someone else take the rap.

To flush the Inner Abuser out of hiding, we ask the question "How do I do to myself what I see this person doing to me?" It's helpful to try a few different phrases, to see what rings for us. Some examples:

- A woman gets angry because someone has ignored her. She can ask herself, "How do I treat myself as if I weren't there? How do I treat myself as if I didn't count? How do I disregard my importance in a crowd?"

- A man is angry at his boss for picking out only the negatives about a report that took two weeks to prepare. In the process of forgiving his boss, he might ask himself, "How do I discount the value of my work? How do I withhold positive feedback from myself? How do I pick on myself? How do I look for negatives instead of positives in myself and others?"

- Someone accuses a woman of "robbing the cradle" because she's going out with a man 20 years younger than herself. She's indignant and angry. "How do I criticize myself for dating someone so much younger?

When the answer to the question becomes clear, the Grownup can ask both Inner Children's forgiveness for allowing the abuse, promise to love and care for them both, and commit to preventing any such behavior from occurring either internally or externally from now on.

Use a Surrogate to Make Communication More Real

Some of the vignettes in this book involve using a surrogate or stand-in to receive the communication that a person needs to deliver to the someone they have decided to forgive. This technique is very useful when the person is dead or dangerous, because it frees the forgiver from any fear of the other's responses. The forgiver's own emotions are all that need attention.

You can set up the surrogacy situation yourself. All you need is someone to play the part of the person you want to forgive, and a place where you have some uninterrupted time. The surrogate's job is to listen and do or say whatever else you ask.

Sit opposite one another and begin telling the surrogate all the things you need to say to the person he or she represents. Don't hold back, but allow it all to flow out, in words, tears, shouting, or pounding.

1. Freely admit to the person all the angry, painful thoughts and feelings you have had about his or her behavior.
2. Confess that you have been collecting and nursing grudges, and that you've used the person's behavior to justify yourself in doing so.
3. Speaking for the offender, the surrogate may at this point say, "I'm never going to change. Are you really going to forgive me?"
4. The next moments are solemn and sacred. Tell the surrogate you are making the decision to let the resentment go and will not be spending more energy on it.

The surrogate, because he or she is merely standing in, needn't reply at all and can let the energy of the communication flow through and out again. Here's a vignette contributed by someone who stood in as a surrogate.

As I arrived in his hospital room, my dear friend Tom asked me to come sit on his bed. He wanted me to know that, after fighting his illness for so long, he had decided to stop all his medications, remove his i.v., and let nature take its course.

He had no illusions about what this meant. He said he was ready now to let go and to embark on the journey that awaited him.

Having known him for many years, and having visited him several times in recent days, I felt comfortable with his choice.

I asked Tom what if anything remained to complete regarding the people close to him so he could leave this life with a light, free heart. After some reflection, he said the only person with whom he was not fully at peace was his mother-in-law, Harriet. He began to tell me all the things he had never been able to discuss with her openly. As he spoke of his pain, he winced, and his voice caught.

I put my arms around him and made a gentle suggestion—since he couldn't talk directly with her about what was weighing on his heart, he could speak to me as though I were Harriet; he could use me as a surrogate.

Immediately he began pouring out his heart, telling her how upset he'd often been at her behavior, and how many fights prompted by her had broken out in his family after she'd left

> *I do not understand why people wait for*
> *deathbed scenes before they will forgive.*
> *Forgiveness is so powerful in the*
> *[physical] healing process that we should*
> *not wait until we are sick to do it.*
> **Maryanne Lacey & Fr. Peter McCall**

their house. Going for broke, he held nothing back. All the pent-up frustration and anger came boiling out. He hadn't been so energized or animated in days, perhaps weeks. His eyes snapped and his voice cracked.

Since I had no need to defend myself as Harriet, I just let him talk till he had said it all.

Then the most remarkable thing happened. Without missing a beat, he went on to say how much he had always loved her, and how sad he was that he hadn't been able to express it in a way that registered with her. He also knew in his heart how much she loved him, too. All his years of resentments and regrets vanished in a sentence or two, and what remained was the presence of God's love in the room.

Forgive God and Pray

We're unsure how much forgiveness is consistently possible using strictly psychological means. Some wounds and associated resentments go very, very deep. It's tough enough to forgive someone who hurt us when we were adult; in most cases, they couldn't have mistreated us without our cooperation. But what about cases where we weren't collaborators in our own abuse? What about the rejecting parent who never did want us? What about the abusing relative who hurt or molested us when we were too small to understand or defend ourselves? What about the society that treated us as not even human? And what about the Creator who allowed life to be so painful for us? The God who took our daddy when we needed him so much?

If you're angry at God but have never told Him so, we recommend you do it. If suppressing your feelings is what's keeping you stuck, expressing your feelings can be extremely healing. And God's big enough to take it. He needs no defending from you or anyone else.

If, after expressing anger at God, you feel no relief, you may be transferring onto Him the image of someone from your childhood, probably a parent. God the Father often looks like our own father. Freudians have known this for a long time. "I never knew an atheist with a good relationship with his father" is one expression of that wisdom. If that's the case, then expressing anger at God is usually a way of evading the issue with one's own parent.

We can say from experience that until you deal with your own father, you won't know whether you actually have any issues with God.

In some of the toughest cases, it seems our pain, rage, and fear have permeated the very cells of our body, putting the decision to forgive well beyond the power of the intellect. Such deep unforgiveness may include a sense that God made a mistake and now disapproves of it. If our parents didn't even want us to be born, we may feel the universe itself is chaotic, with only a thin layer of order stretched over it. The very ground beneath our feet is ever ready to betray our trust.

No mere act of will dislodges such deep trauma. In such cases, forgiveness needs to include forgiving the person(s) for hurting us, ourselves for being hurt, and God for allowing it. Sometimes even after years of work—therapy, self-control, wishing, etc.—our resentment doesn't yield. Then what?

We believe the source of forgiveness is spiritual, which opens up: (1) prayer; (2) healing of memories; and (3) spiritual practice.

> *Prayer.* Actually, the heading on this section is misleading. For us, prayer is the first recourse, not the last resort. We encourage people to begin their own conversation with God, and to pray with us for the power to forgive. "Lord, I don't have what it takes. I'm frightened, angry, hurting, and weary. I'm scared to let down my guard. I'm doing my best, but if You want me to really forgive this person, You'll have to do it through me" is a prayer that God has honored through the ages.

> *Healing of Memories.* Healing of memories offers a way of dealing with profound unforgiveness. We ask God to present the memories that need to be healed, and then for Jesus or our

Higher Power to be there with us as we go back into the memory, to provide the protection and healing power we need for completing the forgiveness process. It has always worked for us.

Spiritual practice. For anyone who can, we suggest setting aside some meditation time each day to do nothing but receive from God. No strings. Listen for the still, small voice within. Imagine yourself sitting across from God and simply allowing yourself to receive. Imagine yourself running and then leaping into God's arms, there to rest safely embraced for as long as you like.

For people who were raised in the church but have drifted away, or for those who have a cordial relationship with Jesus, we recommend taking communion daily.

These processes strengthen us through a connection that bypasses the intellect. That way our busy minds can't interfere with the healing. Here's a story about forgiving God that may prove useful to you if you're wrestling with that issue.

I spent the first five months of my life in excruciating pain and on the borderline of starvation due to a partial blockage of my bowel. This blockage released spontaneously one day while I was crying, but the process was such an agony that I passed out. I woke hours later entirely healed.

Forty years later I remembered the incident. I did some group rebirthing, during which I found myself going back in time. Back, back before birth, back even before conception. I found myself facing Christ and asking him, "Why did You put me in a body of such pain when I knew I had come from such Love?"

The reply I heard from Jesus was "Will you forgive Me?" accompanied by an indescribable Love. The question took me completely by surprise. I had never even thought of forgiveness in connection with my pain. Suddenly the why of it became irrelevant to me, and I knew I was being given a truly free choice.

"Yes, I forgive You." And I was suddenly unburdened of a deep pain and confusion I had carried all those years, of which, until that moment, I'd been unaware.

8

More Forgiveness Stories

The following stories are gratefully reprinted as told or written to us. We have changed the names to protect those involved, but otherwise they have remained as close to the original as possible. We hope they prove helpful to you.

Forgiving Oneself for Failing to Prevent Suicide

In March 1990, Mac and I excitedly set off on a seven-week vacation to British Columbia. Five and a half weeks later, Mac was dead. Suicide.

What happened? Will I ever know? On one level I know what happened. The autopsy verified death by drowning, the final result of severe depression. But what really happened? Neither of us had ever seen depression before. I was the only one who saw his terror. For, unfortunately, while waiting to see doctors, we would both calm down, expecting help was on its way.

After the last doctor visit, Mac revealed, "I'm planning my suicide." Then he actually tried but couldn't do it. When he told me, I felt huge relief and said, "I'm glad you've chosen life." The rest of the weekend was glorious.

Monday morning, depression set in again. That evening, Mac repeated, "I'm going to commit suicide." I replied, "If you do, please don't take our car, please don't take me, and please don't half do it."

That night again he awoke me in great distress and I held him close. "Mac," I said, "I think you'd better take a sedative." After he was asleep I slipped outside to meditate. When I returned half an hour later, the bed was empty.

My moment of shock. I ran to the lake. I called, frantic. No answer. What do I do? Then I saw his suicide note. *I can't take it any more. You've given your all. But your love isn't enough. Love, Mac. P.S. You'll be better off without me.*

My love wasn't enough? Idiot! Why didn't I drag him off to the hospital? Why did I let him do it? Could I have stopped him? *I didn't even try.* I didn't deserve to live.

For the next two years I myself was suicidal. I was haunted by memories of his terror, by guilt, by how he did it, for what I had said—"Don't half do it"—and so he wore his work boots and chains, took sedatives, and walked into the freezing water.

For me to live, I *had* to believe that I was forgiven. I had to believe that he forgave me. I had to forgive myself. I'm sorry Mac, I'm so sorry. I pictured God holding me, loving me in spite of it all. I held myself, crying. I let anyone hold me. And so I have healed. I don't know the "why" for what happened, but I do know that a huge part of my cure has been forgiveness, plus, ironically, the right antidepressant for me that brought my chemistry back into balance.

Now I embrace our cottage, which Mac and I so lovingly created, as a place of retreat for people to be peaceful, quiet, bathed in homey affection, and . . . forgiven.

A Man Forgives His Ex-wife

We fell madly in love. Or at least I did. And so did she, I think. She was so feminine, so emotional, nurturing, relational, magnetic. She looked like the walking fulfillment of all that was unknown to me. It was so mysterious, so fascinating just to be with her. And I felt breathless with the beauty of her body. And I believe the reverse was also true. She wanted to be close to my focus and strength, that ability I innately had to wield power, to go after something in the world and make it happen.

But things began to change. Because we were each so intent on going after the dynamic that the other one had, we lost the ability to express our own unique qualities. The very thing we loved at first we began to hate. Now she was "too emotional" and I was "too power hungry"—the underbelly of what once had been the virtues that drew us together. Neither of us really saw the other. How desperately I needed to be seen and accepted—just as I was. We ended up fighting constantly.

So devastating was the inner loss of my fantasy that I realized if I did not get away from her, I would have killed either her or myself.

The physical separation was the most devastating experience of my life. We had said that we would not let our children suffer, but she used the children and I used money to continue a war we could not let go of.

Underneath, I still had deep feelings for her. I longed to touch her. I longed to connect with that which had given me such life in the earlier days. But when we opened our hearts to one another, the timing was usually off and the next visit to the lawyers completely crushed any possibility. The cruelty of our culture in allowing legal warriors to negotiate the sanctity of a broken relationship is beyond belief.

It is over now. Separated sixteen years, it is time for me to forgive.

So what's to forgive? Everything! First I have to forgive a culture that taught me to make marriage choices on the basis of the "falling in love" experience, an experience I now see as a mild psychosis, full of psychological projections. Second, I have to forgive myself for being such a jerk, so narcissistic, so full of myself and my own needs that I could not see anyone else, especially someone up so close. And third, I have to forgive her for not being what I thought she was. All those years I was saying, "You should be what I think you are, what I construct you to be, what I need."

I forgive you. I forgive me. We are not reconciled in the usual sense of having warm cozy feelings toward each other. Like old Jacob, I walk with a sacred limp. It reminds me of my humanity.

A Woman Forgives Her Ex-Husband for Abandoning Her

Practically overnight, I went from having everything to having nothing. A doctor's wife, I had a beautiful daughter, enjoyed myself in the ultimate playgrounds in the nation, and bought practically anything I wanted, including a maid to clean my house twice a week. Six months later, my husband had moved in with another woman, the bank had foreclosed on our house and repossessed my car, we had both declared bankruptcy, and the one cleaning other people's houses was me!

Why did this happen to me? Look what he did to me, I moaned to myself and to everyone and anyone who would listen. I hated, raged, plotted, and schemed.

97

Today, I have forgiven my husband, mended all the fences that I could, and have, in a way, more than I had before. The road I traveled was forgiveness.

The first step on that road was to change my negative attitude. I had always assumed the victim role, whether I was being persecuted or not. To change this, I resolved to accept that everything that happened to me was for my good, to support me being a winner. Thinking positively took some practice. At first when things went wrong, I went right back to saying I was on God's dump list. But I was actually getting tired of being angry—life was too short.

Eventually, after the divorce and many workshops and much prayer, I asked God to take the anger from me and to help me forgive everyone who had hurt me. It started working. Little by little, I began to mend the bridges that I'd been burning. I called my ex-mother-in-law a few months later to invite her not only to come to my daughter's graduation but to stay with me. We actually enjoyed our time together, and so did my daughter. My daughter and I have had to heal also. I leaned on her more heavily than I should have, and that wasn't fair.

What has enabled me to forgive? New habits are important. I now analyze situations rather than simply reacting in rage (my car has been a teacher for me because it has given me so many opportunities to practice). Time (one day at a) and exercise have also been important medicines. I also speak to myself in love, a lot.

I also practice unconditional love for others. I'm no longer disappointed when people don't come through for me because I no longer expect or demand anything. Nor do I feel controlled by others' expectations in the same way; today I do things not because I feel I have to, but because I want to.

Truly, I have traveled the road from victim to victory.

A Woman Forgives Her Ex-Husband for Battering

Married at eighteen, a "good Catholic girl," my body was calling me to the world of adults. He was twenty-six, handsome, and a man who loved his beer. I was the oldest daughter. I knew how to clean, cook, and run the show. I could make this work. The drinking was a concern—but certainly he would slow down, once married. I could make it work just fine.

One week after the honeymoon, he was five hours late getting home . . . a sick knot filled my belly . . . in he came . . . screaming and ranting . . . fists flying . . . flesh stinging—never any remorse until the day after.

The good Catholic girl had two children in twenty-four months . . . many more drunken fights . . . many broken promises. And no longer did I believe I could make it work.

I left as abruptly as I had jumped in. The only thing I took was a heart full of hate and a head filled with justified resentment. I hated him for never caring, for forcing me to accept that I couldn't make it work.

For years the hate in my heart spilled over and splashed on the men in my life . . . men who had no idea why they were treated so. I paid over and over again as I dragged this hate with me every waking moment. My attention was constantly divided . . . the past had a hold on all present.

I became increasingly aware of my need to find a way to forgive. I had been asking in my prayers and meditation to learn what forgiveness means. I used to believe that somehow I had to be able to forget in order to forgive, but I couldn't stop hating the reality that I had been beaten black and blue by a drunken ex-husband.

Then, during a weekend workshop, I was introduced to the concept of AND not BUT. The leaders gave us the freedom to feel and express all our feelings. To hate my ex-husband's past behavior AND to forgive, I didn't have to let go of anything except the word BUT.

BUT has given me the freedom to acknowledge my past, including my feelings, and to move on. I have been able to contact Walter after ten years to ask him to forgive me for sending hate his way for more than twenty years and to let him know that I forgive him for everything that went on between us. Truly, I am free.

A Woman Forgiving Sexual Abuse

I was 44 when, barely two years ago, the first nightmarish memories erupted of a childhood of wholesale incest and sexual abuse, which started in infancy at the hands of my bisexual mother, her male and female lovers, my stepfather, and others. At Thanksgiving last year, I believed that I had completed the work of forgiving my mother, and I was celebrating that victory. I had no idea there was so much more to go.

Three weeks ago, the memories started becoming available in greater detail. I began to remember further details of certain incidents and realized the shrewd intentionality and deliberateness of all the abuse. I was

When I forgive, I proclaim that God is in charge and that the healing of all people, relations, and situations is coming about. Forgiving myself and others, I am restored to wholeness.

Daily Word

simultaneously shattered and enraged. I was so consumed on all levels that it appeared as though forgiveness had never occurred. Since then, I have been at emotional sea, not only over these new revelations but also over the fact that they seemed to annihilate the prized forgiveness so quickly!

I began to question myself—my integrity, humility, and honesty—as well as what in the hell forgiveness *is* after all! Was it so fragile? Was it a farce? Was it an illusion? Was I a liar? Was I a failure? Was I incapable? From the time I was a little girl I had dedicated myself to an unarticulated path of love . . . as an adult I have openly declared my commitment to the Light, to Love, and to the attainment of the Light through forgiveness, of myself and others. Was I so delusional as to be lost instead of found?

Finally . . . the truth began to emerge from beneath the cloak of anger and grief—I had forgiven each of my abusers after all, but only for their acts in general.

Now it's clear that it's just another layer of repressed consciousness that requires forgiveness and eventually, I know, I will give that gift of love to myself as I did the first time. In the meantime, I am grateful for what I've learned this round:

- Forgiveness doesn't involve the other person as much as myself.

- Forgiveness is an expansion of my heart, an acceptance of the other person's imperfection as a reflection of my own.

- Forgiveness is unconditional ("I'll forgive you IF you never do it again" doesn't cut it).

- Forgiveness is incident by incident.

- Forgiveness means understanding, not approving.

- Forgiveness is Divine and therefore within everyone's grasp.

A Man Forgives Sexual Abuse

My mother was the powerful, demanding one in my family. Full of insecurities, she insisted on love and attention in great quantities. My quiet, reluctant father couldn't fill her void, so she turned to her children.

When my older sister and brother failed her, I, the youngest son, ascended to the throne and became her champion. My mother had been an accomplished pianist and gloried in my musical talents. As I grew older, she called on me to be the loving and attentive spouse she didn't have. Sadly, I mastered the act. She would attack my father's manhood, then cajole me into professing my love for her. I was just a teenager and didn't understand the grinding uneasiness in the pit of my stomach as in quiet desperation I went about trying to please her.

I was initially stunned and then overcome with anguish when as an adult I first realized that I was a survivor of incest. This awareness was part of my recovery process from sex and love addiction. Through subsequent recovery programs and treatment experiences, I discovered the immense rage that seethed beneath my "nice guy" persona. I had gone to great lengths, including becoming an ordained minister, to conceal my shadow self and to prove to the world I was OK. For many years, my wife and daughters paid the price of my passive rage toward women.

In my healing process, I was able to find safe places to fully express my anger at my mother. With the help of many loving people, most especially my wife, Irene, I unburdened myself of this weight and became more capable of honesty and intimacy.

I began yearning to forgive my mother. I heard the promise of forgiveness as the final release from the bondage of both the abuse and the abuser. But just saying it out loud and in my prayers didn't seem to make it happen in my heart.

Then, at a retreat center for personal and spiritual growth, I became familiar with the Goddess ideology. I saw its meaning for women and its significance in transforming our patriarchal culture. I experienced powerful, vulnerable, and safe female energy on that retreat . . . a very loving and healing energy for me. I think it gave me a new vision of WOMAN that went beyond mere mortal flesh. After a written dialogue with my image of this Goddess energy, I cried cleansing tears. I finally knew that there was true goodness in my mother. I wasn't condemned to remember only the hurt and pain. I was able to forgive my mother and accept myself.

Within a year after this transforming experience, my mother died her physical death. I am blessed with being totally at peace with her.

Corrie Ten Boom—Forgiving Murder[10]

It was at a church service in Munich that I saw him, the former S.S. man who had stood guard at the shower room door in the processing center at Ravensbruck. He was the first of our actual jailers that I had seen since that time. And suddenly it was all there—the roomful of mocking men, the heaps of clothing, Betsie's pain-blanched face.

He came up to me as the church was emptying, beaming and bowing. "How grateful I am for your message, Fraulein." he said. "To think that, as you say, He has washed my sins away!"

His hand was thrust out to thank mine. And I, who had preached so often to the people in Bloemendaal the need to forgive, kept my hand at my side.

Even as the angry, vengeful thoughts boiled through me, I saw the sin of them. Jesus Christ had died for this man; was I going to ask for more? Lord Jesus, I prayed, forgive me and help me to forgive him.

I tried to smile, I struggled to raise my hand. I could not. I felt nothing, not the slightest spark of warmth or charity. And so again I breathed a silent prayer. Jesus, I cannot forgive him. Give me Your forgiveness.

As I took his hand the most incredible thing happened. From my shoulder along my arm and through my hand a current seemed to pass from me to him, while into my heart sprang a love for this stranger that almost overwhelmed me.

And so I discovered that it is not on our forgiveness any more than on our goodness that the world's healing hinges, but on His. When He tells us to love our enemies, He gives, along with the command, the love itself.

Forgiving Permanent Physical Injury

I used to walk, hike, ice skate weekly, run after my young daughter. Today, I am a cripple, betrayed by a physician's willful disregard of my health, my requests, my terror, my pain—and my radiologist; by other

> *Write injuries in dust, benefits in marble.*
> **Benjamin Franklin**

physicians who must have known how poorly prepared this man was; by a hospital that chose to allow a man to use their facility who demonstrated three separate times that he didn't know enough to pass the medical boards. After the damage was done, and, despite his blatant violation of the oaths of medical practice, they banded together to invalidate my claims in court. I had a lot to forgive, as you will see, for I live with the reminders every single day.

When I was taken to the hospital with a broken ankle, my regular orthopedist was unavailable, and Dr. H. (for hopeless) took over. I told him I thought the ankle was broken, but after looking at the X-rays, he said to me, "I don't think it's broken, but here's a soft cast & crutches to use over the weekend." Two days later, at 9 a.m. Monday, he called to say there was a small crack. "Come in and we'll put it in a cast.

While I was in the casting room, my regular orthopedist, Dr. A. (for absent) showed up. I pleaded with him to take over the case, but he said Dr. H. was a good physician, had already begun treatment, and he couldn't interfere. *TAKE NOTE: Once a physician has begun treatment, no other doctor will give a second opinion, so be sure you have the doctor you want from the beginning..*

After six excruciating weeks in the cast, my entire foot was swollen, blue, and misshapen. Five months later, I still couldn't walk. Eventually I had to go to a NYC specialist to have the ankle fused, because the calcaneus, the major support bone of the body, had collapsed. After four more months in a cast, my foot and leg were at right angles to each other, with absolutely no movement available, either up and down, side to side, or rolling. My lower leg became like a stick. I was in constant pain.

Sixteen months after the accident, I started asking questions of a malpractice attorney and of other doctors. The more I learned, the worse it got. We brought suit against Dr. H. and, six years later, won the case hands down.

Yet I still limped and hated him for what he did to me.

Then I read in manuscript the book you now hold in your hands. It showed me that I was continuing to let Dr. M. abuse me. I resolved not to give him the satisfaction of hurting me or taking anything more away from me.

The next weekend I returned to Shalom Mountain and realized that Dr. H shattered my foot, not my life, and I'm fine now. I really am fine with it.

9

Summary & Afterthoughts on Forgiving

In the course of producing this book, we have found ourselves humbled daily by our own humanness. Both of us have been beset by irritating, intransigent resentments against others—and ourselves—certifying us as presumptuous indeed to have written a book on forgiveness.

It underscores the truth that forgiveness remains a challenge to everyone—except maybe hermits. Despite periods of goodwill toward all, nobody gets to stay an expert forgiver. No sooner do we begin to pat ourselves on the back for the high degree of enlightenment that we've attained than we find ourselves stuck in some hugely petty attitude that persists in thumbing its nose at us for hours or months.

From where we now sit, we see that all of us persist in using resentment for a wide variety of purposes—to protect ourselves, distance unacceptable reality, distract from our own helplessness, stay connected with someone who's left, buy time to adjust, avoid telling the truth, postpone confronting the real culprit, punish the other, stave off panic and guilt, and a host of other aims. The tendency to blame and to abdicate responsibility is deeply rooted in the human organism, and all it takes to occasion a relapse is a sudden attack of pride.

We have learned yet again that to some degree we are all blind, all deaf, and certainly all dumb. But forgiving gives us new eyes, ears, and tongue. Thus these words by Helen Keller apply to us all:

> *I learned that true forgiveness includes*
> *total acceptance. And out of acceptance*
> *wounds are healed and happiness is*
> *possible again.*
>
> **Catherine Marshall**

The calamity of the blind is immense, irreparable. But it does not take away our share of the things that count—service, friendship, humor, imagination, wisdom. *It is the secret inner will that controls one's fate.* (italics added) We are capable of willing to be good, of loving and being loved, of thinking to the end that we may be wiser. We possess these spirit-born forces equally with all God's children.

In Inner Family terms, we can say that every one of us has Inner Children who believe anger has magical powers to get us what we want or to keep away what we don't want. Without the Inner Grownup's loving attention to their needs, these Inner Children will collect grudges and exact revenge—not realizing the cost to themselves and the other Inner Children. The good news is that, once accessed and reeducated, the Grownup can completely meet the Inner Children's needs, and also relieve them of an inappropriate burden of responsibility for what happened to them.

To put this another way—as we grow in wisdom and self-care skills, we learn to focus more on ourselves to find and forgive the source of our upset. We don't say that all wrongs happen in our own heads, as some courses assert, but we do say that much of the extra energy driving our angry reactions arises from projection. If we're on a path of growing and healing, we learn to own what is ours and leave the rest to God. We become more responsible—appropriately—for what we ourselves allow, and that makes us free. We learn vigilance.

We learn, in the final analysis, that forgiveness means saying "yes" to all that was, is, and will be, instead of "it shouldn't be that way." Forgiveness means choosing to open to all that is in life, including the painful, instead of only what leaves us feeling secure or pain free. It means taking a leap of faith that in the end things will all work out, whether we would have preferred they take the path they did or not.

The forgiveness task is all encompassing; that is, we learn to forgive not only ourselves and others, but life itself and, by implication, the Intelligence that is the Source of life.

Forgiveness, we learn at last, means accepting that suffering is one of our best teachers, and that it is what we suffer that melts away the gristle of our self-centeredness and separation from our Inner Children and from our brothers and sisters around the world.

Recommended Reading

How to Forgive When You Don't Know How was based primarily on personal experience, not on research, so we don't offer you much in the way of further reading suggestions. However, we can recommend the following:

Bishop, Jacqui, M.S. and Mary Grunte, R.N., *How to Love Yourself When You Don't Know How: Healing All Your Inner Children.* Barrytown, NY: Station Hill Press, 1992.

Written for the layperson, this book explains the concept and practice of Inner Family Healing, a self-help therapy process that can be used by individuals, friends, and professionals.

Flanigan, Beverly, *Forgiving the Unforgivable.* New York: Macmillan Publishing Company, 1992.

The cover reads,"Overcoming the bitter legacy of intimate wounds. Far broader in scope than *How to Forgive . . .* this is a readable, scholarly, comprehensive study of forgiveness that should be on every thinking person's desk.

Johnson, Vernon E., *I'll Quit Tomorrow.* New York: Harper & Row, 1980.

A brilliant classic in the field of alcoholism counseling, this book has two sections on forgiveness that are very clear and helpful: Chapter 13, "The Dynamics of Forgiveness" relates a vignette, and "Some Spiritual Dynamics of Forgiveness," a section under Appendix I, explains the process and structure of forgiveness decisions.

Smedes, Lewis B., *Forgive and Forget: Healing the Hurts We Don't Deserve.* New York: Harper & Row, 1984.

An enduring favorite: personal, revealing, beautifully written, and very useful.

Notes

1 For further information, we refer you to the bibliography.

2 Thanks to Steven Karpman for the Drama Triangle concept.

3 Excerpted from the forthcoming book, *Death of a Marriage—Birth of a Woman*, by Lyalya Herold. For the use of the material, we are grateful for the permission of Lyalya Herold, as well as Landmark Education Corporation, which delivers The Forum.

4 See *How to Love Yourself When You Don't Know How*, Chapter 7, "The Myth of the Bad Child: Defusing Inner Sibling Rivalry."

5 Reprinted by permission of Barbara Hoberman Levine, author of *Your Body Believes Every Word You Say*. Published by Aslan Publishing, Boulder Creek, CA 1991.

6 The New English Bible, II Corinthians, 7:8-12.

7 *Daily, Starr*, Love Can Open Prison Doors.

8 Notables who have promoted screaming: Dan Casriel, founder of Daytop and of the New Identity Process; Janov of Primal Scream Therapy; Alexander Lowen of Bioenergetics; and Fritz Perls, who developed Gestalt therapy.

9 The Family Spell is that state of mind in which we find ourselves when an occurrence reminds us so strongly of an intense experience in our past that we can no longer respond appropriately in the present. It affects us as if we were in a trance, and our reactions don't seem properly connected with what is happening in the here and now. It's as if we are looking through a filmstrip at a current event, which we can't see because it is obscured by the images on the filmstrip.

10 From *The Hiding Place*, by Corrie Ten Boom with John & Elizabeth Sherrill. Published by Chosen Books, and reprinted by permission of John & Elizabeth Sherrill.

About the Authors

JACQUI BISHOP M.S., has carried on a private psychotherapy practice since 1982 in White Plains, NY. A graduate of the Foundation for Religion & Mental Health program in Transactional Analysis and Gestalt, Jacqui also worked with Dan Casriel, MD., at the Casriel Institute in the New Identity Process and has done extensive work in a wide variety of other healing disciplines, including rebirthing, massage, Alexander, and other bodywork techniques.

Her recent writings include *The Creative Brain* co-authored with Ned Herrmann; *How to Invest When You Don't Know How* soon to be published; and in the pipeline: *The Holding Book* and *My Boss Doesn't Know What I Do — The Corporate Lawyers Guide to Client Communications.*

MARY GRUNTE, R.N., originated the Inner Family Healing process. She has broad experience in observing behavior in newborns, infants, and children. Her background includes psychiatric nursing in London, England's renowned Maudsley Royal Bethlehem Hospital, followed by delivery room and nursery management in Methodist Hospital in New York. She has further developed the discoveries made in these environments in subsequent work with terminally ill patients and in her psychotherapy practice, which she has carried on in Yonkers, NY. since 1981.

For the past four years, she has led workshops with Jacqui Bishop demonstrating the Inner Family Healing process.

She also wrote and produced *John the Baptist* (music by Bruce Lederhouse), a chancel musical drama that has been produced in several states. She is married to Leon, they have two grown children.

Related Station Hill Titles

How to Love Yourself When You Don't Know How
Healing All Your Inner Children

JACQUI BISHOP & MARY GRUNTE

The notion that each of us carries around an inner child has been widely explored in popular psychology; this groundbreaking book takes the premise one step further, describing an interior model for the individual based on the metaphor of the family. Everyone, say the authors, is really made up of an inner family—several children of various ages and characters, each of who vies for control in one's life, as well as an inner grown-up capable of learning to care for them. The book's aim is to help the reader re-educate the inner grownup to love unconditionally, opening the way for profound healing of psychic wounds.

$10.95 paper, ISBN 0-88268-131-1, 6 x 9, bibliography, index.

Abused
A Guide to Recovery for Adult Survivors of Emotional/Physical Child Abuse

DEE ANNA PARRISH, MSSW

This clear and sensitively written book covers child abuse in all its forms, including types of abuse overlooked by the victims themselves: neglect, deprivation, ridicule, and inappropriate sexual gestures. *Abused* includes a wealth of revealing and highly moving first-person accounts, a program for recovery, a resource directory, and various self-tests to help readers determine if they once were abused and today need counselling or therapy. It includes a parents' guide to behavioral signs of sexual abuse plus the first guide to describe techniques used by therapists to uncover repressed memories. Illustrated with case histories, *Abused* is written for adults who suspect the treatment they received as children still impairs their sense of judgment and well-being today.

$8.95 paper, ISBN 0-88268-089-7, 6 x 9, 150 pages, bibliography, resource guide, index.

How to Break the Vicious Circles in Your Relationships
A Guide for Couples

Dee Anna Parrish

The message of this clear and sympathetic book is that dysfunctional relationships characterized by a predictable pattern of vicious circles—can be healed. Reassuring case histories, drawn from the author's own therapeutic practice, demonstrate why relationships disintegrate, and show how they can be made whole again. Here are proven techniques designed to short-circuit destructive habits. Readers will learn to use "defusers" to keep conflicts from escalating, gauge levels of emotional intimacy and identify barriers to closeness, examine their own levels of communication and quality of listening, use "I" statements to identify problematic issues, and uncover inter-generational patterns of dysfunction. For anyone seeking to improve a relationship or reconnect with a partner—with or without the aid of a therapist—this is essential reading.

DEE ANNA PARRISH, a psychotherapist specializing in family and couple therapy, is the author of *ABUSED: A Recovery Guide for Adult Survivors of Physical/Emotional Abuse*. She lives in Dallas, Texas.

$8.95p, ISBN 0-88268-144-3; 128 pages, 6 x 6 ½.

Another Healing Companion

Good Grief Rituals
Tools for Healing

ELAINE CHILDS-GOWELL

As a psychotherapist with over twenty year's experience, the author
realized that the emotion of grief was not limited to bereavement but was
in fact experienced in an extraordinary range of circumstances, from
natural disasters to the end of a love affair. In this sane, comforting, and
deeply thoughtful book, she offers the reader a series of simple grief
rituals, among them the venting of feelings, letter writing, affirmations,
exercises to act out negative emotions as well as forgiveness, fantasies,
meditations, and more. Adult chidren of alcoholics and dysfunctional
families, victims of incest and assult, and those who've lost a pet, wrecked a
car, or suffered any kind of loss will find that these "good grief rituals"
move them through loss to forgiveness and, ultimately, to gratitude and a
new sense of life.

ELAINE CHILDS-GOWELL, RN, MN, MPH, Ph.D., considers herself a
"spiritual midwife". She has been teaching, and doing psychotherapy for
more than 20 years. She currently works as a Clinical Transactional
Analyst in Seattle, with individuals, couples, families, and groups. Elaine is
known in the Northwest, Canada, Europe and in TA circles generally as a
workshop leader, and particularily for her work relating to Transactional
Analysis with the body.

$8.95p, ISBN 0-88268-118-4; 112 pages, 6 x 6 ½.

Related Station Hill Titles

Emotional First Aid
A Crisis Handbook
SEAN HALDANE, M.D.

Emotional First Aid is the first book to address immediate emotional crisis as distinct from a person's general state of mental health. It deals with grief, anger, fear, joy, and also the complex feelings of parent/child conflicts— emotions that can lead to further withdrawal, illness, or even violence. Clear and extraordinarily well written, this is the frist book to draw on Reichian character analysis to explain how differences in individuals and in specific emotions call for different responses, if one is to be supportive and not invasive. Emotional first aid may precede or prevent therapy in the same way that physical first aid can precede or prevent extended medical treatment.

$9.95 paper, ISBN 0-88268-071-4, 6 x 9, 160 pages, bibliography, index.

Sam Woods
American Healing
STAN RUSHWORTH

This unusual and eloquent book is not about healing technique, but is an extraordinary exploration into the healing spirit. Weaving together prayers and stories, Sam Woods reveals a fascinating world of healings, revelation and discovery through healing, and attitudes toward healing; the book becomes a healing unto itself as we begin to feel and see the way Sam Woods moves through his life. With prayer and praise, illumination and judgment, a healer's view of living today is opened to us, and we see how we are drawn to fall away from the Earth, and how we come back. Sam Woods says, "This book is a join-ing, a listening to the voices of the earth, of the hawk and frog, of the children, of the people. It is a long prayer, a gathering together, a quiet walk into seeing, carrying everything with us as we go, our history, our an-cestors, our sorrow, and our promise."

$11.95 paper, ISBN 0-88268-122-2, 5½ x 8½, 292 pages.